Tony Kushner's
Angels in America

Modern Theatre Guides

Continuum Modern Theatre Guides offer concise, accessible and informed introductions to the key plays of modern times. Each book is carefully structured to offer a systematic study of the play in its biographical, historical, social and political context, an in-depth study of the text, an overview of the work's production history including screen adaptations, and practical workshopping exercises. They also include a timeline and suggestions for further reading which highlight key critical approaches.

Arthur Miller's Death of a Salesman
Peter L. Hays and Kent Nicholson

August Wilson's Fences
Ladrica Menson-Furr

Caryl Churchill's Top Girls
Alicia Tycer

David Mamet's Oleanna
David K. Sauer

John Osborne's Look Back in Anger
Aleks Sierz

Patrick Marber's Closer
Graham Saunders

Samuel Beckett's Waiting for Godot
Mark and Juliette Taylor-Batty

Sarah Kane's Blasted
Helen Iball

Tom Stoppard's Arcadia
John Fleming

Ken Nielsen

Tony Kushner's
Angels in America

continuum

Continuum International Publishing Group

The Tower Building   80 Maiden Lane, Suite 704
11 York Road   New York
London SE1 7NX   NY 10038

www.continuumbooks.com

© Ken Nielsen 2008

British Library Cataloguing-in-Publication Data
A catalogue record for this book is available from the British Library.

ISBN: 978-0-8264-9503-7 (hardback)
       978-0-8264-9504-4 (paperback)

Library of Congress Cataloging-in-Publication Data
A catalog record for this book is available from the Library of Congress.

Typeset by Newgen Imaging Systems Pvt Ltd, Chennai, India
Printed and bound in Great Britain by MPG Books Ltd, Bodmin, Cornwall

Contents

Acknowledgements

Many people have been instrumental while I have been writing this book. First and foremost I want to thank Janelle Reinelt for being an incredibly supportive, understanding, and patient reader, editor and mentor. She made trying to fit this gigantic play into a frame like this seem doable. I could not have done this without her intellectual and moral support.

I thank the series' publisher Anna Sandeman and the incredible Colleen Coalter, both of Continuum Books, whose patience I have tested severely.

I want to thank my students in my THE1041 classes at Baruch College in New York in the fall of 2006 and spring of 2007. Their critical questions, creative thoughts, insightful analysis and engaged ambivalence regarding *Angels in America* as a historical play inform this manuscript in numerous ways. They also willingly and patiently participated in the exercises and their feedback has been invaluable. Thank you guys for repeatedly reminding me that a new generation has grown up after the Cold War without even a cultural memory of those frightful days of the early AIDS crisis and that education is part teaching the world to remember. My dear friend and colleague Jen-Scott Mobley gave me crucial feedback on the acting workshop exercises.

The staff at the Theatre Museum and Archive in Copenhagen, the Royal Theatre Archive in Copenhagen, the Dramatic Library at the Royal Library in Copenhagen, The Schwules Museum in Berlin, and the Lesbian and Gay Newsmedia Archive at Middlesex University, Cat Hill Campus in Barnet have all provided excellent support for doing research on the international performances and the discourse surrounding them. Thank you.

Quotes from *Angels in America* are reprinted from *Angels in America: A Gay Fantasia on National Themes, Part One and Two* by Tony Kushner Copyright © 1993 by Tony Kushner. Published by Theatre Communications Group. Used by permission of Theatre Communications Group.

I also thank my partner David Smedley for his patience with me and love of change. Onwards and Upwards.

General Preface

Continuum Modern Theatre Guides

Volumes in the series Continuum Modern Theatre Guides offer concise and informed introductions to the key plays of modern times. Each book takes a close look at one particular play's dramaturgical qualities and then at its various theatrical manifestations. The books are carefully structured to offer a systematic study of the play in its biographical, historical, social and political context, followed by an in-depth study of the text and a chapter which outlines the work's production history, examining both the original productions of the play and subsequent major stage interpretations. Where relevant, screen adaptations will also be analysed. There then follows a chapter dedicated to workshopping the play, based on suggested group exercises. Also included are a timeline and suggestions for further reading.

Each book covers:

- Background and context
- Analysis of the play
- Production history
- Workshopping exercises

The aim is to provide accessible introductions to modern plays for students in both Theatre/Performance Studies and English, as well as for informed general readers. The series includes up-to-date coverage of a broad range of key plays, with summaries of important critical approaches and the intellectual debates that have illuminated the meaning of the work and made a significant contribution to our broader cultural life. They will enable readers to develop their understanding of playwrights and theatre-makers, as well as inspiring them to broaden their studies.

The Editors:
Steve Barfield, Janelle Reinelt,
Graham Saunders and Aleks Sierz
March 2008

1 Background and Context

This chapter is an introduction to the study of Tony Kushner's *Angels in America: A Gay Fantasia on National Themes*. *Angels in America* consists of two different parts: *Millennium Approaches* and *Perestroika*. This book introduces and analyses both plays. When described together the title *Angels in America* is used and when described individually the separate titles will be used. This chapter explains why the play is important in terms of its theatrical legacy and international importance, gives an introduction to the author's biography, and describes the social, cultural and political background of the play.

Introduction

Angels in America is arguably the most important American play to be produced in the past 20 years. From the moment *Millennium Approaches*, the first play in *Angels in America*, exploded onto the American (and international) stage, Tony Kushner became the most talked about contemporary playwright in America, at the time heralded as both a great revolutionizer and a saviour of the American theatre. The play was, once produced, instantly recognized; *Millennium Approaches* won a Tony Award for best play in 1993; *Perestroika* won a Tony Award for the best play in 1994, and Tony Kushner was awarded the Pulitzer Prize for best drama in 1993 for *Millennium Approaches*. *Angels in America* seemed to energize the critics in a way that the American theatre had not been able to for a long time. In his review of the first complete production of *Angels in America* at the Mark Taper Forum in Los Angeles in November of 1992 the influential theatre critic for the *New York Times,* Frank Rich, wrote that 'Some visionary playwrights want to change the world. Some want to revolutionize the theater. Tony Kushner, the remarkably gifted 36-year-old author of "Angels in America," is that rarity of rarities: a writer who has the promise to do both' (Rich, 1992). Rich's reaction represents a general tendency towards hyperbole in the initial critical reception of *Angels in America*. John Lahr of the *New Yorker*, for example, called *Perestroika* 'a Masterpiece' and claimed that 'not since Williams has a playwright announced his poetic vision with such authority on the Broadway stage' (Lahr, 1993: 133), obviously drawing parallels between Tony Kushner and Tennessee Williams, author of iconic American plays like *A Streetcar Named Desire* and *Cat on a Hot Tin Roof.*

What seemed so appealing about Tony Kushner was the way he galvanized disparate elements and historical movements of and within the American theatre. *Angels in America* is of epic and tragic proportions, not unlike Eugene O'Neill's mammoth plays such as *Mourning Becomes Electra* and *Strange Interlude*, dealing with the inner workings, functions, and histories of individuals, couples and families. At the same time it utilizes the Brechtian elements of the popular political theatre of the 1930s such as Clifford Odet's play *Waiting for Lefty*, and Marc Blitzstein's anti-capitalist musical *The Cradle Will Rock*. Also, Kushner uses elements of Tennessee Williams's lyricism in the creation of characters, particular in Harper who is as lost and delusional as Blanche Dubois in her search for love and belonging (besides, of course, giving Prior the famous line 'I've always depended on the kindness of strangers' from *A Streetcar Named Desire* as a direct homage to Williams). Furthermore, Kushner actively borrows from conventions of musical theatre and theatrical spectacle to create a fast-paced production featuring such spectacles as steel books, flaming letters, a vision of heaven as a decrepit

San Francisco, and, not least, the Angel crashing through Prior's bedroom ceiling.

Another way of judging the importance of a piece of theatre is to look at the controversies sparked by it. *Angels in America* has definitely caused its part of controversy both in terms of censored or contested productions and in terms of scholarship. Historian of gay theatre John Clum, for example, calls the play 'the most talked about, written about, and awarded, play of the past decade or more', 'a turning point in the history of gay drama, the history of American drama, and of American literary culture', and nothing less than 'a turning point for the inevitable, eternal, if turbulent relationship of gayness and theater, the climax of this chapter of its history' (Clum, 2000: 249, 257). Though most often celebrated, scholars have also found the play to be problematic. British critic, Alan Sinfield, though sympathetic to Kushner's politics and project, says 'My misgiving is that *Angels in America* slides into the cloudiness of irony, symbolism, and produndity [*sic*] at moments where clear elucidation would be valuable' and he questions whether or not the hope that is expressed at the end of *Perestroika* rings true. Sinfield asks whether 'a state that has depended on extreme violence in its founding, consolidation, continental expansion and global hegemony can realize, from within the ideology that has shaped it, a future that will be harmonious as well as purposeful' (Sinfield, 1999: 205, 207). Several productions of *Angels in America* have sparked controversy as well, particularly in the American regional theatre. The first major controversy over a production of *Angels in America* took place at the Charlotte Repertory Theatre which staged both plays in 1996 but was met with protests from Reverend Joseph R. Chambers who opposed the performances because of his anti-pornography belief and what he took to be the play's blasphemy. Besides the subject matter as such the Reverend particularly found the simulated sex and Prior's nudity, however brief, to be offensive (Fisher, 2002: 89).

International success

Before *Angels in America* opened on Broadway in April of 1993 *Millennium Approaches* was performed in London in a critically acclaimed production at the National Theatre. This early production was an indicator of the tremendous success that *Angels in America* would have internationally with performances all over the world. It might seem peculiar that a play so specifically American would spark such international interest. It certainly did to Tony Kushner himself who explained to Adam Mars-Jones in an interview at the National Theatre on 24 January 1992; 'The play felt so much addressed to Americans and about America that I never really imagined it was going to go anywhere else' (Mars-Jones, 1998: 20). However, I believe that the international success of *Angels in America* must be seen as a combination of a renewed interest in America after the Cold War, the prevalence of American popular culture throughout the world and the immense theatrical qualities in the play itself. More than any other American play from the last two decades, *Angels in America* intrigued an international audience and offered insights into the world's then only remaining superpower. It offered new insights into a nation that people around the world already felt they knew very well.

Investigating America at a critical point

Angels in America appeared at a time where the world-order that had been in place since the Second World War seemed to be crumbling. The Berlin Wall had fallen in 1989 creating a symbolic end to the Cold War, the Soviet Union disappeared almost overnight and in the USA Reaganism was displaced as Bill Clinton took office and promised a new America in 1993. At the beginning of the 1980s Ronald Reagan had been elected President of the USA using the slogan of 'morning in America', promising a renewed optimism, and exorbitant consumerism combined with lower taxes and supply-side economics. Tony Kushner describes this era as being essentially greedy and without compassion, understanding or equality for minorities or the poor. He says: 'Nineteen eighty-four through 1985 was a horrible, horrible time. It really seemed like the maniacs had won for good. What Martin says in *Millennium* now seems like a joke that we can all snigger at, but at the time I just wrote what I thought was most accurate', that is, that there would never be a Democratic president again and that there would be a permanent Republican majority on Capitol Hill (Savran, 1996: 306–307).

It is against the backdrop of late Cold War society that *Angels in America* must be read. The play investigates an American society plagued by egoism, consumerism, greed, AIDS (or Acquired Immune Deficiency Syndrome), hypocrisy and loneliness as a vantage point from which to create an almost Brechtian parable about the very nature of the American nation. After all, the play's subtitle is 'a gay fantasia on national themes'.

About the play's author

In 1996 Tony Kushner said about *Angels in America* 'I think it's my best play because I started writing about my world' (Savran, 1996: 313). Compared to some of his earlier plays, *A Bright Room Called Day*, for example, is set in Weimar Germany, Kushner really did describe the world he saw and lived in directly in *Angels in America*. The play takes place in New York City, where Kushner lived and lives. Five of its characters are gay men, as is Kushner. Several of its characters are Jewish, as is Kushner. Louis is an ardent believer in some form of socialism, radical democracy and American liberalism, as is Kushner. Though I am not arguing that *Angels in America* should be read solely as an autobiographical play, knowing a writer's background can help put the work in perspective. While doing so it is important to realize that there is no direct correlation between art and life, between the writer and his work, and that no particular character is the mouthpiece of Tony Kushner. As a matter of fact, critics disagree on which character, if anyone in particular, represents Kushner's own views.

British critic Christopher Bigsby has aptly described Tony Kushner as 'a man wandering through a snowstorm of influences, his head tilted back to the sky. Where others might see contradictions, he sees a kind of harmony, unlikely, perhaps, but real enough given his upbringing' (Bigsby, 1999: 86). It is clear, as Bigsby points out, that there are markers from Kushner's biography in his works and that the world he writes about in *Angels in America* is one that brings together the personal (as drawn from his personal life and experience) and the political (as it is seen in the play's scathing indictment of America under Ronald Reagan in the mid-1980s). One of the play's great strengths lies exactly in the combination of the personal with the political. In his attempt to define his own political theatrical practice, Kushner also points to the connection between his personal history, his politics and his theatre when he says 'The genesis of my politics is no loftier, no less mundane, nor more free of family drama than the genesis of my theatrics' (Kushner, 1997: 20). The importance of eliminating the perceived gap between the personal and the political is evident in Kushner's writing. Theatre is always, to Tony Kushner, both personal and political.

As a gay, socialist, Jewish, white man Tony Kushner shares characteristics with many of the characters in *Angels in America*. Though raised in Lake Charles, Louisiana, a southern state in the USA, Tony Kushner was born in New York City on 16 July 1956. His parents, whom he describes as 'New York-New Deal liberals transplanted from New York to the Deep-South' (Kushner, 1997: 20), were both classically trained musicians and fervently interested in both arts and politics. His parents had inherited this interest in culture, politics and their interconnected nature from their parents and is something that Kushner finds closely related to Jewish culture in general. In Jewish culture Kushner identifies an 'insatiable curiosity, skepticism, pessimistic optimism, ethical engagement, and ardent pursuit of the millennium' (Kushner, 1997: 20). These traits are most prominently displayed in the play in Louis's guilt-ridden pursuit of his own life. Besides coming from a Jewish liberal family, Kushner's politics were sharpened through experiences of 'mild anti-semitism and not-so-mild homophobia' while growing up Jewish and gay in the American South (Kushner, 1997: 20). This experience also runs through a later work by Kushner, the musical *Caroline, or Change* which is set in Louisiana and describes a young Jewish boy's relation to his black Nanny.

Kushner became interested in the theatre early on when his mother became the leading lady of the Lake Charles Little Theater, Louisiana. He describes her as an actress who, despite being an amateur, was of 'considerable emotional depth and power, a real tragedienne' (Kushner, 1997: 19). Among other parts she played Linda Loman in *Death of a Salesman* and Anne Frank's mother in *The Diary of Anne Frank* (Savran, 1996: 293). Kushner describes how watching her act when he was between the ages of 5 and 9 enthralled him because of the power of her acting and the nature of performance itself. The effect his mother's acting had on her audience was impressive, inspiring and created in the young Kushner a sense of 'total identification' (Kushner, 1997: 20). From hindsight, Kushner also describes how the theatre represented a sort of free space. In the safe and fictional space of the theatre the performance of a character potentially sets one free through the liberation of not having to be oneself. Kushner describes growing up as a deeply closeted child and young man who had 'decided at a very early age to become heterosexual' but who also sensed that the theatre, with its potential for disguise and transformation, could offer a free space in which to become something else (Savran, 1996: 293). This notion of being able to escape one's own identity through perform-ance runs through the central, ultimately liberated, characters in *Angels in America*; Prior and Belize both found (and find) escape in doing drag, while Harper escapes into fantasy and imagines herself in different versions – a migrating Mormon mother, a woman in Antarctica and being pregnant, for example.

In an essay titled 'American Things' Kushner describes freedom and the necessity of living free. He also, however, describes his own family's political belief system in a description of the family's Passover Seder. The religious/political belief system that Kushner grew up within was one that drew connections between the ancient suffering of the Jewish people and contemporary struggles, between ancient and modern exploitations, between an ancient lack of civil rights and a modern one. The liberalism that Kushner's parents installed in him, and one that in turn influences his world view and writing, is 'the aggressive unapologetic, progressive liberalism of the thirties and forties, a liberalism strongly spiced with socialism, trade unionism and the ethos of internationalism and solidarity' (Kushner, 1995: 5). In this combination of religion, identity, politics and an intense perception of historical perspective we can find much of the belief system undergirding *Angels in America* with its broad scope, historical critique and belief in progress however painful and difficult.

Tony Kushner came back to New York City in 1974 to attend Columbia University from which he graduated with a Bachelor of Arts degree in English Literature in 1978 (Fisher, 2002: 14). Kushner's time at Columbia proved to be formative in terms of developing his thinking and politics; influenced by faculty and fellow students, Kushner found his world changing. He began studying the German philosopher Karl Marx and found himself inspired by Marx's dialectic thinking and anti-capitalist critique. It was also at this time that Kushner was first introduced to the German thinker, playwright and director Bertolt Brecht who is a foundational inspiration for Kushner's work. Reading Brecht's text *Short Organum for the Theater* and Brecht's play *Mother Courage and Her Children* (which is one of Kushner's favourite plays and which he has translated for the Public Theatre in New York City) changed his view of the theatre and opened up a world of politically engaged theatre for him (Savran, 1996: 294). It was also at Columbia that Kushner first read the German philosopher Walter Benjamin whose thesis on history would later supply the idea of the Angel for *Angels in America*.

While at Columbia University, Kushner also started going to the theatre. While still seeing more traditional Broadway theatre, Kushner also recalls seeing performances of Richard Schechner's production of *Mother Courage*, and performances by other New York theatre artists such as The Wooster Group, Spalding Gray, Lee Breuer, Richard Foreman and JoAnne Akalaitis. The late 1970s was an inspiring and vital time for the American theatre in its combination of traditional playwriting and a more experimental downtown scene developing a non-narrative, visual, physical and at times non-verbal theatrical style. Two years after graduating from Columbia, Kushner decided to apply to New York University's (NYU) Tisch School of the Arts for a master's degree in directing wanting to work with the director Carl Weber who had worked with Brecht at the Berliner Ensemble in the 1950s. He was accepted to NYU and while at Tisch, Kushner started writing plays in a wide variety of styles and genres and co-founded a theatre company called 3P Productions, using the three p's in politics, poetry and popcorn (which later became The Heat and Light Company) to produce his own and other plays. However, as Kushner graduated from NYU in 1984 he was experiencing 'a very, very black time' (Bigsby, 1999: 91; Fisher, 2002: 15; Szentgyorgyi, 1998: 11).

'The very black time' was characterized by the loss of a relative, a close friend's serious car accident, the disintegration of 3P Productions, Carl Weber's exit from New York, and finally, perhaps most importantly, President Ronald Reagan's re-election. The re-election of Ronald Reagan, whose politics, strategies and rhetoric, Kushner found appalling, was an indication of the state of the nation to Kushner. Besides later setting *Angels in America* during this dark time, he also began work on a new play, *A Bright Room Called Day*, that would draw historical and political parallels between the last days of the Weimar Republic and Ronald Reagan's America.

A Bright Room Called Day was initially produced by the Heat and Light Company at Theatre 22 in New York City in 1985. In 1988 it was produced in London, where it was met with rather harsh criticism, and in 1991 it opened at the Public Theater in New York. Much like *Angels in America*, though on a different scale, the play interweaves the private lives of a group of people with events in history. It takes place within the Berlin apartment of Agnes Eggling, a middle-aged actress, and centres on a small group of friends. The play follows the disintegration of this group under the rising pressures of Adolf Hitler's Nazi Party. As the political climate changes the group must face the question of what to do next, not unlike the question that faces Prior in *Angels in America*. What do you do in the face of catastrophe? Exile is the course chosen by most of the characters in *A Bright Room Called Day* though not for Agnes, who stays in her apartment. Interspersed with the scenes of the play we find so-called 'disruptions' by a young woman named Zillah who directs a critique of contemporary American politics directly towards the audience. In a historical parallel, Zillah has fled Ronald Reagan's America and the power of the Republican party in an attempt to reconnect with history and to wake America from its chosen amnesia; by theatrical coincidence she lives in Agnes's old apartment. In the end Zillah decides to leave Berlin and go back to America to re-engage in the fight for change. In this early play one can clearly see the outlines of the theories and styles of the two plays *Millennium Approaches* and *Perestroika* that were to consume much of Kushner's time for the next many years.

Following the enormous success of *Angels in America*, Tony Kushner has become one of the most talked about playwrights in the American theatre. In the years following the play he has written a number of new plays: *Homebody Kabul* and the musical *Caroline, or Change* being the two best known, and worked on the screenplays for Steven Spielberg's *Munich* and the HBO adaptation of *Angels in America*.

The social, economic and political context

Though *Angels in America* takes place over the course of 3 months during the fall and winter of 1985–1986 and its immediate context is that of the United States under the Reagan administration and the early years of the AIDS epidemic, it frames and draws on a much longer historical frame, primarily that of the Cold War and its consequences. The Cold War was the term given to the protracted ideological battle between the US and the Soviet Union after the end of the Second World War. It was not 'hot' – actual warfare – but it was strategic and brutal in both countries, and it structured hostilities between the two nations and much of the world for over 40 years. It is this binary world-order that the play takes place within.

The play draws clear parallels, through the historical characters of Roy Cohn and Ethel Rosenberg, between Reagan's America and its AIDS crisis and America during the 1950s, McCarthyism, and the second Red Scare. The play is full of references to current and histori-cal events: the medieval plague, the Mayflower, the founding of America and the philosophy of radical individualism, the visions of Joseph Smith, early Jewish immigration to the US, the Mormon migration West, and people such as McCarthy, Reagan and a wealth of others. As the late days of the Weimar Republic serve as a historical parallel in *A Bright Room Called Day*, the structure, politics and cul-ture of the Cold War is used to parallel the 1985 state of the United States of America in *Angels in America*. Daryl Ogden comments on this when he writes 'Kushner portrays Reaganism polemically, as a version of Neo-McCarthyism' (Ogden, 2000: 243).

If we consider the eulogy by the Rabbi at the opening of *Millen-nium Approaches* to be a prologue of sorts, it is actually Roy Cohn who opens the play – showing off his power to his protégé, Joe. In that scene he single-handedly represents the disingenuous nature of politics and functions as a symbol of American Republicanism. He is neither interested in change nor the people, but only in his own power and its preservation. The corrupt execution of Ethel Rosenberg that he helped achieve is the ultimate sign, to him, of the power he has wielded in the world. Through the confrontations between Roy Cohn and Ethel Rosenberg, Kushner highlights the essential position of the Cold War as background for the play, making the 1950s a parallel to Reagan's 1980s. The fear of Communism, symbolized in Roy Cohn's relation to Senator Joseph McCarthy's prosecution of alleged Communists, creates a parallel to the Reagan administration's treatment of minorities such as gay people and the administration's reaction to AIDS. The white straight monolith that Louis and Belize discuss in the coffee shop scene is constructed in the play as being the Reagan administration; a continuation of McCarthy's binary philosophy and approach to society is seen in his words, 'if you want to be against McCarthy, boys, you've got to be either a Communist or a cocksucker' (Courdileone, 2000: 521).

America under Ronald Reagan

There are widely different opinions about the presidency of Ronald Reagan. Supportive scholars praise Reagan for his optimism, his tax-cuts, his transformation of Social Programs, his foreign policy and the enactment of supply-side economics. Critics blame him for the exact same policies. It is beyond doubt however that the election and re-election of Reagan changed America in several ideological ways and that 'the Democrats of 1989 and 1990 sound a bit more Republican than they did in 1980 or 1984' as one scholar reflecting on the period put it (Berman, 1990: 3).

Ronald Reagan was elected on the slogan of 'Morning in America' often invoking the image of letting America be the shining city on the hill. Reagan promised in his first election campaign to restore pride and optimism in America following the 1970s' pessimism based on the tremendous damage done by the Vietnam War, race riots, oil crises, international terrorism and the Iran hostage situation. The Reagan/Bush administration (1981–1989) cut taxes as part of their so-called 'supply-side economic theory' whose central premise is that if the individual is given more money (i.e. pays less taxes) this will create a dynamic economy as the money will be put back into the economy in the form of consumption. Critics of supply-side economics claimed that it was nothing but a way of making the rich richer and the poor poorer. Thomas E. Mann, for example, says: 'The poverty rate is no lower and by some measures is actually higher than before. There are some people in this country who have been left behind' (Mann, 1990: 23). In order to slim down the welfare state, which the Reagan Republican party judged as being out of control, they cut social programs by $700 billion while giving a $50 billion tax-cuts, and increasing defence spending 27 per cent. However, his transformation of American society, known as the Reagan Revolution, was not just an economic decision but part of Reagan's overall project of restoring America to its former self. In his farewell address to the American people, Reagan described his own presidency, not as a revolution (which had been the common description), but as a rediscovery of 'our values and our common sense' (Berman, 1990: 5). In this way, according to Reagan himself, the 1980s was a reconstruction of a nation that had gone astray during the 1960s and 1970s with the increased liberation of minorities and experimentation with other forms of living of those years. The gay community had experienced tremendous personal and sexual liberation since the riots at Stonewall Inn in New York City in June of 1969 and it was partly this increased sexual freedom, manifested through visibility, that Ronald Reagan campaigned against with his project of restoring America by emphasizing issues of morality, religion and family values in social and cultural policies. Reagan's focus on religion and restoring the traditional American nuclear family proved detrimental to his administration's reaction to AIDS.

AIDS in 1980s America

Two events in the spring and summer of 1985 changed America's thinking about the disease (AIDS) that was killing thousands and thousands of American citizens: the opening of Larry Kramer's play *The Normal Heart* and the death of Rock Hudson. AIDS had been killing particularly gay men and intravenous drug users in America since the beginning of the 1980s and had by 1985 become a regular epidemic. Although the Center for Disease Control estimated in June of 1985 that 11,010 Americans had contracted AIDS and that 5,441 had died, the Reagan administration had yet to address the topic or to initiate or allocate money for research. Then on 23 July 1985, Rock Hudson, American film star, he-man and heart-throb publicly admitted that he had AIDS thereby giving the disease a public face. Until then he had maintained, much like Roy Cohn in *Angels in America*, that he had liver cancer. Rock Hudson going public with his disease, though not his sexuality, created an early watershed moment in the history of AIDS from which point on AIDS could no longer be kept a secret 'gay' disease (Shilts, 1987: 575–582). Having not yet addressed the topic in public, Reagan mentioned AIDS in a press conference in 1985, but the Reagan administration did not give a major policy address on the AIDS crisis publicly until 1987.

It is clear that if the Reagan administration had focused on AIDS research and prevention earlier the epidemic might have taken a different course. Though officials from the Department of Health and Human Services asked for increased funds to conduct research and prevention and did not receive any, they publicly maintained that they had sufficient funding thereby undermining the nation's research and treatment potential. This is indicative of the administration's reaction to the crisis and the nation's dying citizens. When AIDS first struck, Reagan and the Republicans had just been elected on their social conservative platform and they were in no way eager to publicly react to a crisis affecting, at the time, primarily gay men, who, besides trying to cope with the crisis, were repeatedly scapegoated by many of the political right. During this period the white house physician reports that Reagan thought 'it was measles and it would go away' (Rimmerman, 1998: 399).

It can be hard to fathom today the devastating nature of AIDS on the American gay community and the consequences of the disease, enormous fear combined with despair that nothing seemed be done about it. Through the inaction, the official policy of ignorance, gay men were treated as people with no rights, as amoral people who had brought this upon themselves, and as discardable. In an interview with the magazine *Body Positive,* Kushner looks back on the 1980s and discusses the representation of AIDS in his play:

> I really was astonished in the 80s at the extent to which people believed – and it wasn't only Reagan, though he's culpable because he was elected to be a leader – the way in which society as a whole believed for a long time – believed that we deserved to die because we had sex with each other. (Pacheco, 1998: 59)

That Kushner is not exaggerating can be seen from how the conservative movement in America, the people backing the Republican Reagan administration, spoke about the disease as a lifestyle problem indicating that since, in their belief, homosexuality was a choice, well, so was AIDS. Patrick J. Buchanan who was then, and is now, a Republican commentator put it sarcastically in his first column addressing the crisis: 'The poor homosexuals – they have declared war upon nature, and now nature is exacting an awful retribution'

(Shilts, 1987: 311). *Angels in America* then takes place within a gay community ravaged by confusion, fear, silence from the administration, and, not least, blame.

If gay activism had been on the downhill at the beginning of the 1980s with much of the gay minority believing that liberation had indeed to some degree been won – though, as Roy Cohn points out in the play, it hadn't had much legislative success – AIDS radicalized gay culture into taking action in the face of devastation. Larry Kramer, whose play *The Normal Heart* put the epidemic on stage in 1985, had also been instrumental in founding the Gay Men's Health Crisis in 1982 – an organization supplying practical help to people with AIDS while at the same time a lobbying on their behalf. Years later, in 1987, Kramer was also one of the initiators to a much more visible organization dealing with questions of AIDS politics and activism: ACT UP (an acronym for AIDS Coalition to Unleash Power) (Epstein, 1996: 219–221). With ACT UP the gay community refused to be silenced anymore; in fact one of the slogans read 'Silence = Death', written on a black background featuring a pink triangle visually connecting what they claimed to be a genocide against gay people with the Nazi prosecution and execution of homosexual people. The formation of ACT UP was important for Kushner as he began writing *Millennium Approaches* because of the way the organization showed its anger and political defiance in the face of crisis. ACT UP (and the later formation of the group called Queer Nation) insisted on gay and queer visibility and civil rights in a way that *Angels in America* also does. The project of queering America, central to the play, was suddenly gaining ground in post-Reagan America.

2 Analysis and Commentary

This chapter is a study of *Angels in America* both as a dramatic text and as a performed play that has excited comment and provoked analysis. Beginning with a thorough plot summary that sketches out the main actions of the play, I undertake a broader analysis of its characters, influences, images, themes and key scenes.

Plot summary

It is nearly impossible to summarize *Angels in America* without reformulating its sprawling nature and episodic quality. *Millennium Approaches* is structured in three acts, consisting of nine, ten and seven scenes. *Perestroika* is structured in five acts, consisting of six, two, seven, nine and ten scenes followed by an epilogue. While reading the play, or watching a performance of it, one can become overwhelmed by the rapid speed of the scene changes and the switches between the real and the imagined, the natural and the supernatural, the past and the present. Kushner uses several different techniques for structuring the play: split scenes, fantastical elements and a significant sub-plot constituted by Roy Cohn. The use of split scenes allows Kushner to juxtapose the personal and the political, the real and the fantastic, and the relations between characters. The split scene technique is used to indicate simultaneity and the intertwined nature of the characters' lives and struggles. In the split scenes we see several worlds happening at once, and a reader or spectator is able to draw parallels between the two situations. The fantastical elements bring the play out of its domestic realism and allow a reader or spectator to access a grander vision of the society and world that the characters exist within. The sub-plot of Roy Cohn serves multiple purposes; it brings attention to the hypocrisy and fundamental homo-erotic nature of power in a patri-archal society while also historicizing the play, allowing Kushner to construct a parallel between 1950s Cold War America and the present. It is helpful to keep these structural elements and Kushner's deliberate and strategic use of them in mind while reading the play. The section below outlines, in some length, the action of the scenes as a guide for reading the play.

Millennium Approaches

Act 1

All the acts in *Angels in America* have their own titles indicating, in a Brechtian fashion, what the main subject or function of the act is. In *Millennium Approaches,* Act 1 in nine scenes is called 'Bad News', and introduces the reader to the characters, the main themes and central conflicts of the play. It takes place in October and November of 1985 in New York City.

Scene 1 is a monologue by Rabbi Isidor Chemelwitz who is speaking at the funeral of Sarah Ironson, Louis's grandmother: It functions as a prologue to the play. *Angels in America* thus opens with a funeral indicating that something is dead; a way of being in the world disappears with this individual death. The rabbi points out how Sarah Ironson was the last of a generation who made the great journey from Europe to America in search of a better life. She is an example of the migration that America is founded upon. He describes America as a melting pot where nothing melted and continues by saying to the descendants of Sarah Ironson that they actually do not live in America. Instead these descendants, accord-ing to the rabbi, carry with them their grandmother's Lithuanian or Russian or any other ethnic identity, and it is this identity that shapes their lives, not America. America is a fictional construction in which all sorts of ethnic and religious identities strive to create a certain American identity. This opening scene introduces the central relationship between migration and roots, fixed and fluid identities, stasis and change. The deceased Sarah Ironson was an example of migration in search of hope and progress; something the disillusioned Rabbi declares no longer exists.

In the following short scenes we are introduced to the central characters of the play: a homosexual couple, Louis Ironson and Prior Walter; a heterosexual Mormon couple, Harper Amaty Pitt and Joe Porter Pitt; and the character of Roy Cohn. In scene 2 Roy Cohn is meeting with Joe Pitt in his office from which he exercises his power. He simultaneously talks on several phone lines and with Joe, who he clearly sees as his protégé. He offers to arrange a promotion for Joe, who is a chief law clerk, to the justice department in Washington. Although Joe sees this as a tremendous chance, he has to consult his wife. The following scene introduces us to his wife Harper, talking to herself and Mr Lies, who is a recurring hallucination for Harper in her Valium-induced haze. She has premonitions that something will happen and presents visions of an imminent apocalypse. In the following scene, Louis and Prior are talking outside the funeral home where Sarah Ironson's funeral took place. Prior reveals that he has AIDS and that he is afraid that Louis will leave him now. The revelation of Prior's disease is followed by the first split scene of the play.

In this scene Louis is talking to the Rabbi in a cemetery about the guilt he feels for not going to see his grandmother when she was sick, and how he fears his own reaction to Prior's disease. Intertwined with this, Joe and Harper are discussing the possibility of moving to Washington, which Harper does not want to do, revealing her tremendous anxieties and her current emotional problems.

In the next two scenes the characters become connected. Scene 6 takes place in the men's room at the courthouse where both Joe and Louis work. Louis is crying by the sink as Joe enters. Joe shows compassion towards Louis, who reveals that his 'friend' is sick. Furthermore Louis complains about the Reaganite lawyers who work at the court house while Joe, being one, defends them. Louis teases Joe that he is gay and Republican and Joe denies being gay. The scene ends with Louis kissing Joe on the cheek. Following this, in scene 7, Harper and Prior share a hallucination; Prior is having a feverish dream and Harper another hallucination. Prior is in drag applying his make-up at a large make-up table, but the drag doesn't cheer him up, and he is breaking down as Harper arrives. After trying to figure out how it is they can appear in each other's dream/ hallucination, Harper claims that they are at the very threshold of revelation, and that she can see that despite his sickness there is a part of him that is not affected. Prior on the other hand lets Harper know that her husband is homosexual. As Harper disappears and Prior removes his make-up, a large grey feather falls down and a voice from above proclaims that he must 'look up' and 'prepare the way' (41).

Following this is a second split scene in which both couples are having discussions. Harper is trying to confront Joe with the information Prior gave her in their hallucination. He is fighting what he contends is sinful, deep within him. At the same time Louis is outlining a somewhat theoretical discussion of justice and the after-life, while Prior talks about the progress of his disease, his fear of dying and of being abandoned. Louis begs Prior to not get any sicker. Throughout the play Louis uses theoretical discourse whenever he is uncomfortable or unsure of how to react. Here he uses it to avoid discussing Prior's disease and its consequences.

In the following scene Roy Cohn is in his doctor's office. His doctor informs him that he has AIDS, but Roy Cohn, who is a closeted homosexual, refuses the diagnosis. He claims that he has liver cancer and forces the doctor to agree.

Act 2

Act 2 consists of ten scenes and takes place in December 1985 and January 1986. It is titled 'In Vitro' (Latin for 'in glass') which is a scientific term for conducting an experiment outside of a living organism, for example, in a test tube.

The two first scenes show Louis and Prior and then Harper and Joe. The act opens with Prior being violently sick on the floor of his apartment. After calling an ambulance Louis holds Prior on the floor while praying to God for strength to deal with the situation. The same night, in scene 2, Joe walks in on Harper sitting in the dark. She tells him that she is pregnant, and that she thinks he should go to Washington alone. He will not leave her, but she informs him that if he will not leave her, she will leave him. It seems that everything is breaking apart. Following that, in scene 3, Prior has been admitted to the hospital and Louis is talking to the nurse, Emily, explaining Prior Walter's somewhat peculiar name – meaning the Walter before this one. Louis realizes that he cannot deal with Prior being sick and leaves the room. Scene 4 is a split scene in which Joe and Roy are at a bar in Manhattan while Louis is cruising for sex in Central Park. Joe is trying to explain to Roy what his relationship to Harper is like, and why he cannot leave her. Simultaneous with their conversation about the relationship between fathers and sons, mentors and mentees, Louis is in Central Park, attempting to engage in rough sex, wanting to be hurt in a masochistic simulated daddy/boy relationship. The scene ends with Louis leaving the guy in Central Park after their aborted attempt at sex, while Roy tells Joe that he is about to die of cancer.

The following scene takes place 3 days later in Prior's hospital room. We are presented with Prior's African-American friend Belize, a former drag queen who is a nurse. Prior tells Belize about the Voice and complains about Louis's leaving. After Belize leaves, Prior talks to the Voice again asking if she is coming to take him, but she says that she is a messenger instead and that she will come to begin the great work.

Scene 6 takes place during the second week of January. Roy and Joe are having lunch with Martin Heller, who works for the Reagan administration, discussing the Republican revolution of the 1980s and how Joe could make a difference in the Justice Department in Washington. Martin Heller and Roy illustrate how nepotism works in Washington and Roy challenges Joe's ethics when he asks him to go to Washington to protect Roy from disbarment. It is revealed that Roy is faced with disbarment from the New York State Bar Association and wants Joe to go to Washington and exercise power on his behalf. Joe can only promise to think about it. Scene 7 is set the same afternoon on the steps of the Hall of Justice in Brooklyn where both Louis and Joe work and now accidentally meet. They continue the conversation from the bathroom scene in the first act, centring comically on gayness and Republicanism. Louis worries about Reagan's children and characterizes the new decade and its people as 'greedy and loveless and blind. Reagan's children' (80). This is followed by a short scene in which Joe calls his mother, Hannah, in Utah in the middle of the night to tell her that he is homosexual. She rejects him by telling him to go home and forget the call.

Scene 9 is set the following morning and is a split scene between Prior's hospital room and the Pitts' apartment in Brooklyn. Joe has come home to tell Harper that he is leaving, and Louis has come to tell Prior that he is going to move out. Prior accuses Louis of being incapable of love. Harper calls on Mr Lies to take her far away. Both are left at the end of the scene.

The last scene of the act is set in Salt Lake City, Utah. It is sunset as Hannah Pitt is talking to her friend and real estate agent about selling her house so she can move to New York City to save her son. Unlike the early Mormons Hannah is migrating back East instead of out West.

Act 3

Act 3 consists of seven scenes and takes place in January 1986. It is titled 'Not-Yet-Conscious, Forward Dawning'.

At the beginning of scene 1 Prior is having a nightmare, wakes up, turns on the lights and is met by a man in the costume of a thirteenth-century British squire, which in medieval England was a young man aspiring to become a knight. The man, called Prior I, is Prior's ancestor who died of the plague during the outbreak in the 1200s. The two are visited by another ghost, another Prior, this one called Prior II. He is dressed as a seventeenth-century Londoner, and he also died of the plague – this time during the 1600s. After describing the individual plagues that they died from, they inform Prior that they have been sent by the Angel to prepare him for her arrival. Obviously the appearance of the two ghosts lets us see Prior's disease, AIDS, in relation to other historical epidemics such as the black plague, indicating both the seriousness with which Kushner approaches AIDS and the historical perspective the audience should bring to the scene.

Scene 2 is a split scene. In a very different environment than the mysticism of the previous scene Louis and Belize are discussing politics in a coffee shop, while Prior is at an outpatient clinic going through a check-up with his nurse, Emily. As the scene opens Louis starts into a long monologue on the topic of why democracy has been successful in America. He outlines a liberal theory that radical democracy has the possibility to grow and spread uniquely in America and that America, ultimately, is a symbol of progress in the world because of its unique constellation of race, immigration and optimistic belief in progress. However, during the lengthy and wordy monologue, Louis starts contradicting himself. While arguing against Reaganism, Louis points out that power, not tolerance, is the ultimate goal, and equating power with politics, he argues that it is ultimately politics itself and not race that defines what it means to be American. Wanting to argue for pluralism leads him to argue that there is no American monolithic culture – except, perhaps, the monolith of 'white straight male America' to which Belize dryly answers 'which is not unimpressive, even among monoliths' (96). As Louis's politically contradictory monologue goes on, Belize gets increasingly impatient and angry, accusing Louis of being completely insensitive to racial questions in America. When Louis turns the conversation to Prior and claims that love cannot be ambivalent, Belize retells what he claims is the plot of a novel of interracial love in the years before the American Civil War, and whose heroine, a white girl, utters those same words to her black lover. Obviously Belize is sarcastically making fun of Louis comparing his American romanticism with that of the southern Belle's, who falsely believes that her love and good intentions alone can conquer racial differences. Simultaneously with this discussion Prior is receiving a check-up from his nurse. When the nurse points out that he doesn't seem to be getting worse, which is good, Prior voices his feeling that something terrible is going to happen. At the same time his nurse starts speaking in Hebrew, but denies that she even knows Hebrew afterwards. In a blaze of light a great book appears on stage, opening to show the flaming Hebrew letter Aleph, representing a male god. As suddenly as it appeared, it disappears again. The scene goes back to Belize and Louis who are trying to make up after the fight. Louis expresses his enormous sense of guilt over leaving Prior, but Belize refuses to give him comfort.

In the following scene, scene 3, we meet Harper, who we last saw when Joe announced that he had to leave, in Antarctica. It snows and she is dressed in a beautiful snow suit. Antarctica represents a space where, according to Mr Lies, the shattered can find refuge. Harper has thus retracted to an emotional hallucination where she can no longer be hurt by Joe and her unsatisfied craving to be loved.

Meanwhile Hannah Pitt has made her way to New York City from Utah. We meet her in the burned out landscape of the South Bronx. In a comic encounter with a disturbed homeless woman Hannah informs us that Joe has not picked her up at the airport and so she got on the wrong bus. After not getting clear answers to her questions, Hannah ends up yelling at the woman who, much to Hannah's surprise, gives her directions to the Mormon Visitors

Center in Manhattan, where the homeless woman sometimes seeks shelter. Hannah takes off to the centre.

That same day, in scene 5, Joe has come to see Roy to let him know that he cannot go to Washington. Roy expresses his extreme disappointment that this prodigal son has let him down because of integrity, for which Roy has nothing but scorn. Roy expresses that being nice will get you nowhere, and that his proudest achievement was the execution of Ethel and Julius Rosenberg, which he made sure took place by pressuring the judge. Joe is horrified by this admission of illegal and unethical activities. The two have a physical encounter – somewhere in the wasteland between an erotic embrace and a fist-fight – and as Joe leaves, Roy is on the floor calling for his assistant to come in. However, the ghost of Ethel Rosenberg shows up instead announcing that 'the fun's just started' as she calls an ambulance for Roy. Roy claims that he is not afraid of her, death or hell, because he is immortal. He says that he 'forced my way into history' to which Ethel answers 'History is about to crack wide open. Millennium Approaches' (118).

Later that night Prior is in his bedroom watching the ghost of Prior I in horror. This time the ghost is dressed in robes and carries leaves of palm. Prior II appears as well, dressed alike, and the two dance around proclaiming that the messenger is near. Suddenly Louis appears as a romantic dance tune is heard. Prior's pain magically disappears and the two dance until, suddenly, the ghosts and Louis disappear and Prior is left alone. The sound of wings is heard.

The last scene of the play is a split scene between Prior's bedroom and Central Park. Prior is alone in his room, afraid, listening to the sound of wings. Meanwhile, in the park, Louis and Joe meet and reach out to each other. Prior, in his bed, is listening terrified while the sound of wings approaches. Suddenly he is overwhelmed by a strong sexual feeling and, as the light and sound changes, an angel crashes through his ceiling, floating above the bed, announcing 'the great work begins: the messenger has arrived' (125).

Perestroika

❧ **Act 1**

Like *Millennium Approaches,* the acts in *Perestroika* have subtitles. Act 1 takes place in January 1986, as an immediate continuation of *Millennium Approaches*, and is titled 'Spooj', meaning sperm or ejaculation, as explained by Prior in scene 4.

The act opens in the hall of the Deputies to the Kremlin. Aleksii Antedilluvianovich Prelapsarianov, the world's oldest living Bolshevik, is giving a speech on the issue of change. As the party moves to reform the Soviet Union the old Bolshevik fears that the grand theory, Marxism, will be abolished as well. Until a new theory has been created change must stop as change without theory will undo society, he claims. After the speech we return to Prior's bedroom where the Angel is suspended above his bed. As with *Millennium Approaches* the first scene functions as a prologue to the play indicating the central struggle between stasis and change structuring the play itself.

In scene 2 we are back with Harper. Unlike in the Antarctica scene in *Millennium Approaches*, Harper is now dressed in the outfit she wore when fleeing the apartment. She is now dirty and dishevelled; she enters dragging a pine tree. It turns out she has been walking around in the Brooklyn Botanical Garden in Prospect Park thinking about her life with Joe. Suddenly Joe appears to let her know that he is having an affair and Harper asks him to come back. In the end she is arrested. Following this is a short scene, scene 3, during which Hannah arrives at the Pitt apartment where she learns that Harper is in custody.

Scene 4 takes us back to Prior's bedroom. The ceiling is now intact and it looks like nothing has happened. Prior calls Belize, who is on duty at the hospital, to let him know of his dream. The meeting with the Angel gave Prior an orgasm, giving the act its name. Though he is scared he is also uplifted, full of joy, or hope. As the two are singing 'Hark the Herald Angels' Roy Cohn's doctor arrives wanting

Belize to admit Roy to the AIDS ward. Belize, reading the slip, says that the oncology ward is elsewhere. He calls Prior and lets him know that Roy Cohn has been admitted with AIDS. In the following scene, scene 5, Belize enters Roy's hospital room to care for a frightened Roy. Roy spews forward racist remarks, but Belize lets him know in no uncertain terms that he is in charge of the painkiller and this makes Roy behave. Roy claims that he is not afraid of pain and starts philosophizing on the historical alliance between Jews and black people. Belize, who is once again subjected to a white person's dubious theory on race, ignores him. Frightened Roy asks if he will die soon, to which Belize answers in the affirmative. Recognizing that Roy Cohn is after all a gay man, Belize, in an act of solidarity or compassion, tells Roy not to let his doctor give him radiation and to use some of all his supposed power to get his hands on a new AIDS medicine still in trial (AZT). Roy calls and bribes Martin Heller, the justice department lawyer who Roy and Joe met with earlier, into securing some for him.

The last scene of the act takes place in Louis's new apartment in Alphabet City on the Lower East Side of New York City, where Ethel Rosenberg and many Jewish immigrants lived. The apartment is messy and dirty. Louis and Joe arrive from the park where they met earlier. Joe is suddenly uncomfortable and doesn't want to have sex, but Louis seduces him by asking him to just use his body, his nose and his tongue.

Act 2

Act 2 takes place 3 weeks later in February 1986. Its title is 'The Epistle (for Sigrid)'. An epistle is a letter or a piece of formal writing sent to an individual or a group. The Sigrid referred to in the title is the actress Sigrid Wurschmidt who was a member of the epic theatre company, the Eureka, in San Francisco where *Millennium Approaches* had its first production. The part of the Angel was written for Wurschmidt who, unfortunately, died of breast cancer.

Ellen McLaughlin, who played the Angel in several productions, dedicated her Broadway performance to Wurschmidt.

In scene 1 Prior and Belize are outside a funeral parlour on the Lower East Side. They have just attended a funeral for a mutual friend, a famous New York drag queen. Prior has begun dressing in a strange somewhat biblical style of a cape, hood and scarf. Belize wants him to lighten up, but Prior retells the story of his meeting with the Angel, of how he has received a book and a prophecy. This scene bleeds into scene 2 which is a complicated flashback.

We are back 3 weeks earlier, at the time of the Angel's arrival. In lyrical tones the Angel informs Prior that she is the Angel of America and she orders him to remove the implements claiming that he has been told in a dream where they would be. This is obviously a reference to the visitation that Joseph Smith (1805–1844), the founder of Mormonism, had from the angel Moroni in 1823. He was the first American prophet and founded the first essentially American religion based on the angel's revelations. Smith and his followers were initially met with scepticism and hostility and experienced a series of violent persecutions. Following Smith's death by an angry mob, the Church, led by Brigham Young settled in Salt Lake City, Utah. Scholars have pointed out how Mormonism is fundamentally based in an optimistic belief in human progress and America as the promised land in which to search for it and that the migration West, besides being a necessity, became part of this search. The Mormon Church views the 'traditional' family as foundational to the life of the individual and to society as such. Critics of the Church maintain that Smith never had a visitation and that the Church is overly repressive of sexuality and supports sexism. Unlike Smith, in this staging of Mormon theology, Prior, on the other hand, has no idea what the Angel is talking about, so after consulting with a Voice she lets Prior know that the implements are under the kitchen tiles. Prior refuses to obey the orders, but the Angel blasts the floors open and forces Prior to retrieve the implements. He returns with an old leather suitcase and retrieves a pair of spectacles with rocks instead of lenses, an image consistent with Smith's visitation. He puts them on and is thoroughly terrified. He also removes a book with bright steel pages, but before opening the book, the Anti-Migratory Epistle, he asks why he always becomes erotically aroused when she is near, and the Angel answers, 'Not Physics but Ecstatics Makes the Engine Run' (173). Both get incredibly erotically aroused and have a strange sort of intercourse, climaxing violently. While the Angel speaks in her lyrical pattern, Prior explains in asides to Belize. He explains that the angels are basically incredibly erotic bureaucrats, who can carry out any order, but who have no imagination and, therefore, cannot create change.

Through this visitation we are presented with a myth of creation in which God, by creating humans, also created the possibility for change and randomness. The angels, however, cannot handle this change and just want the world to stop. Progress must stop and, according to the angels, humans must cease migrating and inter-mingling. It turns out that God, bewitched by humans, left heaven on 18 April, 1906 – the date of the San Francisco Earthquake – and has not been back since. The Angel wants Prior, as the prophet, to stop the world from moving forward, which, as Belize points out, is impossible. After cradling Prior and stating her demands once more the Angel and Prior's bedroom disappears, and he is back on the street. Belize refuses to believe this visitation ever happened, but Prior has started to believe that he is, indeed, a prophet.

Act 3

Act 3 also takes place in February 1986 and is titled 'Borborygmi (the Squirming Facts Exceed the Squamous Mind)'. Borborygmi is plural for borborygmus, which is the rumbling sound from the stomach occasionally occurring when a human or an animal digests food.

Scene 1 takes place a month after the end of the first act and a week after the end of act 2. It's 5 a.m. in the morning. It is a split scene.

Joe and Louis are in bed in Louis's apartment. Louis is sleeping, but Joe is awake watching Harper who is in their Brooklyn apartment. Taking the lead from the previous act, this one continues the breakdown of the distinction between previously separate realities, so Joe can watch Harper and she can enter Louis's apartment. Hannah enters the room where Harper is standing carrying a clean dress and a pair of shoes. As Hannah exits again, Harper enters Louis's apartment and talks to Joe, asking him if he is happy, telling him that he cannot save Louis, and that he is turning into her. After she leaves Louis wakes up, and Joe admits, to Louis's horror, that he is a Mormon.

In scene 2 Roy Cohn is on the phone in his hospital room. He is furiously refusing to hand over his documents to the disbarment committee. As he goes into a painful stomach spasm, Ethel Rosenberg arrives. Belize enters with a pill tray to give Roy his medicine. As a reference to Roy's telephone scene in *Millennium Approaches*, Roy attempts to carry on several conversations at once: with Belize, on the phone, and with Ethel, whom Belize cannot see. Roy throws Belize's pills against the wall and boasts that he has his own supply of AZT which, indeed, he does. Though he has much more medicine than he will ever need, he will not give Belize any and hates his 'kind's' sense of entitlement. After a longer argument full of racial, anti-Semitic and homophobic slurs. Belize wins by offending Roy after which he gives in and lets Belize have a bottle. He takes three and leaves. Ethel, on the other hand, stays until she has to leave to watch the disbarment committee hearings.

Later the same day we find Harper sitting in the diorama room at the Mormon Visitors Center where Hannah works. Prior, who claims to be doing research on angels, enters with Hannah, who attempts to start the diorama of a Mormon family migrating to Utah, but it does not work. Harper informs Joe that the husband in the diorama looks like her husband. In a reference to their shared hallucination scene in *Millennium Approaches* they both seem to believe that they have seen each other before. Suddenly the diorama starts working and Harper and Prior are treated to the early history of Mormon migration to Utah. Harper keeps a running commentary to the diorama until suddenly Louis appears in the diorama having a discussion with Joe, who is the father dummy, about how he cannot believe that Joe is actually a Mormon. As this happens Prior starts breaking into the conversation as well. Harper informs Prior that Louis appears every day in the diorama, although, as she somewhat annoyed points out, he has nothing to do with the story. Louis demands that Joe leaves with him, which he does, after which Harper closes the curtain. Believing that he is losing his mind Prior breaks down while Hannah enters blaming Harper for his tears. She pulls the curtains open and the mannequin in the diorama is now a real dummy. After Prior leaves, Harper asks the mother in the diorama for advice feeling that her 'heart's an anchor' (201). The formerly silent migrating mother suddenly speaks to Harper urging her to 'Leave it, then. Can't carry no extra weight' (201), after which she leaves telling Harper to come along.

Later that afternoon Joe and Louis are sitting on Jones Beach. Their discussion turns to Joe's Mormonism, which Louis still cannot believe. In an attempt to prove himself, Joe starts removing his temple garment – his Mormon underwear – but Louis makes him put it back on. Louis cannot distinguish Joe's Mormonism from his Republicanism and as Joe tells Louis he loves him, Louis tells him that he wants to go back and see Prior. Louis walks away. They both, however, remain on stage.

On the night of that same day, in scene 5, Roy is on morphine in his hospital room. Roy thinks Belize has come to take him away and, in his morphine high, asks him what the other side is like. Belize offers him a vision of a broken down San Francisco overflowing with flowering weeds, full of gender confusion and racially mixed people. As Belize says, 'Race, taste, and history finally overcome' (210). As Belize leaves, Ethel enters to keep watch. They all remain on stage.

In the next scene Harper and the Mormon mother are standing by the Brooklyn Promenade. Looking at the Manhattan skyline the Mormon mother sees nothing but towers filled with fire, proclaiming it to be the great beyond, and that change on a human level is always incredibly painful. As all begin to sing 'Bring Back My Bonnie to Me' Louis leaves Joe at the beach and goes to call Prior.

Act 4

Act 4 also takes place in February and is called 'John Brown's Body'. John Brown was a white abolitionist who spoke for, and participated in, armed uprisings against slavery in America. He was hanged on 2 December 1859. The title refers to a popular marching song used by the Union forces during the American Civil War. It is sung by Roy Cohn on his death bed in scene 9.

Compared to the interconnected nature of the scenes in act 3, act 4 keeps a more traditional division between separate worlds. The first scene is a split scene between a meeting of Louis and Prior in the park and Roy's hospital room where Joe has come to see him. Roy is clearly worsened, though he is doing his best to disguise that fact. He proclaims himself to be the heart of modern conservatism. Joe was worried that Roy wouldn't want to see him anymore after he didn't take the job in Washington, but Roy asks him to kneel besides his hospital bed, which he does, and Roy blesses him. In a parallel situation, in the park, Louis is asking for Prior's forgiveness but without receiving it. Prior confronts him with his knowledge of Joe. Back in the hospital room Joe tells Roy that he has left his wife and has been living with a man for a while now. Roy gets furious, crawls out of bed, removes his IV drop and attacks Joe. Belize intervenes and Joe leaves. Back in the park the discussion between Prior and Louis is still on the topic of Joe being a gay Republican Mormon lawyer and how Louis let Prior down by moving out. Prior will not accept Louis's pain or his sorrow unless he can see bruises on the outside.

The following scene, scene 2, is a much more farcical scene. Belize and Prior have sneaked into the court-house in Brooklyn where Joe works and are sneaking around to find him. Prior tells Joe that Harper was right that he does indeed look like the Mormon dummy, but then immediately denies that he knows Harper. Prior claims to be a prophet and utterly confuses Joe, then leaves. Belize pops in and Joe recognizes him as Roy's nurse. As Belize and Prior leave, Joe confronts them and they pretend that Prior is a mental patient.

At the beginning of scene 3 Louis is sitting alone by the Bethesda Fountain in New York where he has asked Belize to meet him. He wants Belize to tell Prior that he is no longer seeing Joe. Belize informs him that Joe is having sex with Roy Cohn. Incredulous, Louis accuses Belize of just saying this because he is in love with Prior. Belize doesn't fall for the attack and just lets Louis steep in his own guilt before saying that if he had ever bothered to ask he would know that Belize has his own boyfriend. He points out how Louis is all about big ideas and nothing else. It turns to a discussion of the idea of America, referencing back to their previous discussion from the coffee shop, and Louis's love of it. Belize says that he hates America, because it's nothing but grand ideas and theories. To him America is like Roy Cohn: 'Terminal, crazy and mean' (228).

Scene 4 takes place at the Mormon Visitors Center where Hannah is working as Joe enters. He has come to ask about Harper, but Hannah does not know where she is. He realizes that he should not have called his mother about his homosexuality. As Joe exits, Prior enters asking if Joe is her son. Prior is sick and asks Hannah to take him to the hospital, which she does.

In the following scene, scene 5, Harper is standing in the rain back at the Brooklyn Promenade. Joe enters and Harper has premonitions of Judgement Day because of the signs that the other characters are seeing: Prior seeing angels, the coming alive of the Mormon diorama, and Hannah selling her house and migrating across the continent. Joe says that he has come back to her.

Scene 6 is another short scene. Prior has been admitted to the
hospital where he is being cared for by Emily. Hannah is also
present. Hannah and Prior discuss Prior's vision which he fears is
a sign of insanity. Hannah shares her Mormon belief that visions
do happen and that the angel Moroni was real. Prior asks her if
prophets ever reject their visions, their calling. Hannah confirms
this leading him to ask her to stay by his side through the night.
Thunder is heard and, since he is becoming erotically aroused, he
knows that the Angel is once again on her way.

The following scene, scene 7, takes place in Harper and Joe's apartment in Brooklyn. They have just had sex and Harper asks what he
thinks of while they have sex. She suspects he thinks about men and
he confirms her suspicion. When Joe answers that he does not see
anything when he looks at her, she realizes that the truth has finally
set her free.

In the following scene, scene 8, Joe comes to see Louis in his
apartment in Alphabet City. Having learned from Belize in scene 2
that Joe was an intimate of Roy Cohn's he has started reading the
decisions Joe has written for Justice Wilson. Based on the decisions,
which he finds show a perversion of justice, he attacks Joe for being
a hypocritical, homophobic, self-hating, Republican Mormon. Joe
ends up beating Louis. Louis tells him to leave.

In the last scene of the act, scene 9, we are back in Roy's hospital
room where Roy is on his death bed singing 'John Brown's Body'.
Roy knows he is dying and is elated that he is still a lawyer. Being
a lawyer was the bedrock of his identity. However, Ethel Rosenberg
arrives from the disbarment committee hearings to inform him that
he has been disbarred. Ethel tells him that she had come back to see
if she could forgive him, which she cannot, and to see him die
a more terrible death than hers. Despite being unable to forgive
she sings in Yiddish for the dying Roy when he asks her to. After
gloating that he finally made Ethel Rosenberg sing, Roy Cohn dies
repeating the words from act 1, scene 2, that he wants to be an

octopus, so he could talk on several phones – the symbol of his influence and power.

Act 5

Act 5 also takes place in February of 1986. It's titled 'Heaven, I'm in Heaven', referring to the Irving Berlin standard 'Cheek to Cheek' first sung by Fred Astaire in the 1935 movie *Top Hat*.

Taking place that same night, scene 1 is set in Prior's hospital room where Hannah is sleeping in a chair next to him. Prior wakes up announcing that the Angel is on her way when suddenly a trumpet sounds and Hebrew letters are seen all over the walls. The Angel arrives, this time dressed in black, and looks terrifying. Prior, wishing to reject his prophecy, wants the Angel to go away and take the steel book with her. Not knowing what to do, he takes advice from Hannah, who says to wrestle the Angel. Prior wrestles the Angel in a violent match (during which the Angel tears a muscle in her thigh). During the match a light from above indicates that heaven has opened, and a ladder falls down full of burning Alephs. Prior accepts that he must go and ascends to heaven. After he goes to heaven the Angel turns to Hannah. When the Angel spreads her wings, the room becomes red and Hannah kneels in front of her in a mixture of desire and fear. The Angel kisses Hannah on the forehead giving Hannah an enormous orgasm.

Scene 2 is set in heaven, which looks like San Francisco after the 1906 earthquake. It is a prelude to scene 5. Prior is dressed in his prophet robe and carrying the large book. He runs into Harper, sitting on a box caressing Prior's cat, Little Sheeba, that ran away when he got sick. The two discuss the anatomy of loss and how to live, as humans, knowing that loss is integral to life. The scenery falls apart and the inner chambers of heaven open.

In scene 3 we are back in Roy's hospital room at 2 a.m. in the morning. Belize has brought Louis in to steal the leftover AZT from Roy Cohn's cabinet and say Kaddish, an Aramaic prayer which is part of mourning rituals in Judaism, for Roy Cohn. Louis who is black and bruised from being beaten up by Joe accepts to steal the medicine but refuses to say Kaddish for Roy Cohn, who he thinks is the embodiment of evil. Belize, again in an act of solidarity with the homosexual Roy, suggests that perhaps the Kaddish is where love and justice, the two elements that Louis discussed in the coffee shop scene in *Millennium Approaches*, can finally meet. Not knowing the words well Louis has trouble beginning the prayer. Behind him, Ethel Rosenberg stands up and says the Kaddish with him.

Scene 4 is set in the Pitt apartment in Brooklyn where Joe enters with his suitcase. He is coming back, expecting to meet Harper, but it is the ghost of Roy he meets. Roy kisses Joe softly on the mouth, tells him to follow his love, and leaves. In scene 5 we are back in heaven with Prior. The scene is the council room of the Continental Principalities. The angels, looking at an ancient map of the world, in a room filled with papers and books, are listening to an old radio announcing that the Chernobyl catastrophe will take place in 62 days. The angels are horrified by what will happen, but their discussion dwindles into a comical conversation about the nature and science of the radio itself. Prior and the Angel of America arrive and Prior tells the angels that he wants to return their book, that he will not stop progress. Modernity, characterized by progress, migration, and motion, is what humans are and desire, according to Prior. Prior refuses to follow the reactionary angels in their desire to sit around and wait for God to return. The angels point out that the world seems to be spiralling into chaos and destruction. Prior agrees and, yet, he says: 'We live past hope. If I can find hope anywhere, that's it. That's the best I can do. It's so much not enough, so inadequate but . . . Bless me anyway. I want more life.' (267), after which he leaves. The following scene, scene 6, which is optional in production, takes Prior back to the streets of heaven where he meets the Rabbi from act 1, scene 1 and Louis's grandmother.

In scene 7 Prior descends from heaven into his hospital bed. Hannah is in the bathroom and Belize is sleeping in a chair, but wakes up. Prior has been struggling in his sleep but has returned to life able to tell his experience, thinking that it was all a dream. Louis enters with the bag of AZT telling Prior, again, that he wants to come back.

Scene 8 is the last split scene of the play. Louis and Prior are in Prior's hospital room. Joe and Harper are in the apartment in Brooklyn. This scene is a reversal of act 2, scene 9, in *Millennium Approaches*, where Louis and Joe announced to Prior and Harper that they were leaving. Here, instead, Prior and Harper tell their partners that they cannot return to where they were, that things have changed. Harper demands Joe's credit card before taking off. Prior admits that he loves Louis, but that does not change his decision not to let him come back. Prior and Harper have changed as characters and cannot go back to stasis – the world only spins forward after all.

Scene 9, another optional scene in production, is a monologue by Roy Cohn from his position in Hell. Standing waist-deep in a smouldering pit he offers to represent God for whatever he is being sued for. Roy Cohn, always the lawyer.

In the last scene of the play, scene 10, Louis, Prior and Joe, remain on stage from their previous scene. Harper appears above them, suspended in mid-air, on her way to San Francisco. She shares her insight that through pain and suffering we progress. She says 'Nothing's lost forever. In this world there is a kind of painful progress. Longing for what we've left behind, and dreaming ahead' (275).

Epilogue

The epilogue takes place in February 1990, 4 years after *Perestroika*. It is titled 'Bethesda' referring to the Bethesda Fountain in Central Park in New York City. The Bethesda Fountain was unveiled in 1873 as a tribute to the lost soldiers of the Civil War. It refers to the

Biblical story of the angel who touched the Bethesda pool and gave it healing powers to cleanse whoever bathed in it. Prior, Louis, Belize and Hannah are sitting by the fountain. Belize and Louis are arguing about world events: the fall of the Berlin Wall and the following reformation of Eastern Europe, Gorbachev's politics and philosophies, the end of the Cold War, the Palestinian case, and so forth. As they continue in the background, Prior, going blind but happy to be alive, speaks directly to the audience about the angel of the fountain, the biblical story of the cleansing powers of the water she touches. Though the fountain doesn't flow at the moment of the scene, Prior knows that it will flow again. In a concluding speech Prior makes the case that progress and change are both possible and good.

Character analysis

In more traditional plays than *Angels in America,* there will often be a particular singular protagonist. *Angels in America*, though built around the history of two central couples, can be said to have a more collective protagonist, as we follow eight characters weave in and out of each other's lives. This obviously complicates the notion of a central character as they all relate to each other and drive each other's lives. Critics disagree on who the 'central character' of the play is, which corresponds with the critique of American individualism, particularly in the age of Reagan, that Tony Kushner puts forth in the play. Centring the play in a group of characters, a collective protagonist, allows Kushner to highlight the play's message of communitarianism in a structural way. Discarding the traditional single protagonist furthers the play's critique of Western, and, particularly, American individualism.

Prior

Kushner describes Prior as a man who occasionally works as a club designer or a caterer and who lives quite modestly on a small trust fund. In other words Prior is a man who does not hold a steady job, who travels in circles often thought of as constituting parts of the so-called gay lifestyle, and who is a character clearly outside the Reagan administration's definition of a moral life. Theatrically, Prior is a victim. He has lost his cat, he is diagnosed with AIDS, his boyfriend runs out on him, he is visited by a strange conservative angel, he has been chosen as a prophet, fears he is going crazy and finally is taken to heaven. In face of all this, however, in spite of being scared, he refuses to be victimized by ultimately refusing to submit to the Angel's demand that he stops the world from spinning forward. Instead he insists on having more life.

Kushner explains Prior's name in a twofold way. Louis explains his name to the nurse Emily, when Prior is first taken to the hospital. She wonders why anybody would be named Prior Walter and Louis explains that Prior is from an old family. That the Walters go back to the Mayflower and beyond clearly establishes Prior as a central character not just to the play, but to the very formation of America. In this way Prior can be seen as embodying the central WASP (white Anglo-Saxon protestant) foundation in American culture upon whom questions and concerns regarding racial, sexual and religious identity are projected throughout the play. The name Prior Walter, however, also refers to Walter Benjamin as a 'ghosting' presence in the play.

What also becomes clear by way of the epilogue is the way in which Prior becomes the white male gay unifier of the diverse people of America that the 'white male straight monolith' has failed to create. In the epilogue we see Louis, Belize and Hanna (a white Jewish socialist, a black effeminate man and a proud Mormon mother) discuss world matters until Prior magically tunes them out to offer his message of hope for America. Allen J. Frantzen, who offers an interesting analysis of Prior's character and the importance of his being Anglo-Saxon, points out how the Angel picks Prior as a prophet because of his long American and Anglo-Saxon ancestry, but also how he is able to refuse her because he is infected with AIDS.

The 'plague' that, in different ways, killed the two former Priors then ends up not killing this Prior, but instead gives him the possibility to reject reaction, to reject stasis, and go on (Frantzen, 1997: 134–150). Also in the last words of the epilogue, Prior blesses the audience and repeats the Angel's words that 'the great work begins'. In the end, then, the victimized gay man with AIDS, having rejected the reactionary angels, becomes the progressive American Angel. In his study of the play, Ranen Omer-Sherman points out the extent to which Kushner fathoms Prior in religious terms – casting him, the AIDS victim, the modern outsider, as the prophet. This, according to Omer-Sherman, links to the understanding in several liberal denominations of Judaism that 'prophesy' should always be understood in relation to an inclusive mission of social progress (Omer-Sherman, 2007: 78–98).

Louis

In his interview with Tony Kushner, David Savran states that Louis, though not being the main character and not being the author's voice, is the one character that is central to its structure. All the other characters are tied together (and untied, one could add) through Louis and his actions. Dramaturgically this is an important observation (Savran, 1996: 306). It also, I believe, points to the psychology of the character. As the events of the plays unfold and the world gets more and more chaotic Louis is at the centre of the storm, part of which he has created, and part of which he must now endure. He is, to use Savran's formulation, 'the unmistakably ambivalent, ironic Jew' embodying in some way the combination of Judaism and politics with which Kushner grew up. Louis combines the religious element of the play with the political sphere. Throughout the play we follow Louis as he struggles on through his own indecision, his tumultuous emotional life, and his confused politics. As the world breaks down around him, it seems that the only thing Louis has to cling to is his belief in his own radical politics. The scene key to understanding Louis as a character (and his political function in this political play) is his discussion with Belize in the coffee shop. The scene is as comical as it is enlightening as to the conflicted nature of Louis's life and beliefs. Though Louis might not be the author's voice, he does dominate the play's political discourse throughout the play. When we find a political discussion it is usually with Louis as its centre-point with either Joe or Belize as more or less unwilling participants. Louis's private confusion in his own politics then ultimately leads to the play's somewhat muddled, or as David Savran calls it, ambiguous, politics (Savran, 1997: 13–39). According to Savran, Louis questions several of his own opinions in the course of the play, becoming 'the spokesperson for liberal pluralism, with all *its* contradictions' (Savran, 1997: 30).

When talking to the Rabbi in the cemetery about leaving Prior and what the scriptures have to say about someone like that, Louis describes himself as someone who has a sense of the world, that it will change for the better with struggle, maybe a person who has this neo-Hegelian positivist sense of constant historical progress towards happiness or perfection or something, who feels very powerful because he feels connected to these forces, moving uphill all the time . . . (31)

It is exactly Louis's neo-Hegelian belief in progress that gets tested throughout the play as Louis's inner and outer worlds collapse under the weight of catastrophe. American scholar David Krasner also points to the centrality of this line in his thorough analysis of the development of Louis's character in relation to the notion of progress (Krasner, 2006: 98–111).

Harper

As the plays' one main female character (if we think of the two couples and Roy Cohn as the central characters) Harper has often been criticized as a vague, strange, pill-popping and insane character showing, to some degree, Kushner's disinterest in her situation and existence outside of the plays' gay universe. One could claim that Harper exists more as a sounding board on which to display the consequences of the gay men's actions. Though initially describing Harper as 'Joe's wife, an agoraphobic with a mild Valium addiction' Kushner rejects the criticism of Harper as insane. In an interview with Bruce McLeod he rejects that Harper is crazy or has any problems with reality (McLeod, 1998: 81). On the contrary, Harper has an incredibly vivid imagination, which is clearly seen in the first scene she shares with Prior. This is the hallucination in which Harper and Prior share the 'threshold of revelation'. In this scene both Harper and Prior are seeing reality more clearly than they normally do, despite the fact that they are indeed in a hallucinatory stage. In this way Harper's psychological escapes allow her to see clearly what she cannot see in reality.

Harper is a tremendously unhappy person wishing to be touched by her husband. She has had the incredibly bad luck of being a sexually active Mormon woman who is married to a gay man who does want to, or cannot, have sex with her without closing his eyes and pretending she isn't there. This is at the bottom of Harper's unhappiness. Despite her Valium-induced hallucinations Harper is an extremely lucid character – both when hallucinating and in reality – such as when she says to Joe 'In the whole entire world, you are the only person, the only person I love or have ever loved. And I love you terribly. Terribly. That's what's so awfully, irreducibly real. I can make up anything but I can't dream that away' (56).

In Harper's refusal (or inability) to be normal, in her defiance of the odds, in her Valium-induced clarity, in her outspoken longing for sex (actually, Harper seems far more sexual than all the gay men that interrupt her life), she becomes the ultimate resistance against Reagan's America. Harper's conversation with the Mormon mother concerning the painful nature of existence shows this. Harper is also the one who is set free in the end and escapes to San Francisco. She, not Louis, gets the final neo-Hegelian words that 'In this world, there is a kind of painful progress. Longing for what we've left behind, and dreaming ahead' (275). Far from being the left over or, as Alan Sinfield puts it, 'discarded', female part, Harper proves to be central to the play's staging of the powers of imagination in progress but is, as Natalie Meisner points out in her feminist critique of the play, ultimately removed from the very world in which progress takes place, suspended, as she is, in thin air (Meisner, 2003: 180; Sinfield, 1999: 205). Meisner claims that Harper is constructed to stay, as a basically comical figure, within the theatre of the ridiculous while the boys move on into the realm of fabulous. While Kushner does not believe that Harper is crazy, she does function as the most clearly pathologized character, which several feminist critics have also noted. However, in the play's litany of oppressed people I believe that Harper also serves as a reminder of the ongoing oppression of women so often produced by pronouncements that women are hysterical and psychologically weak.

Joe

Joe is the only straight main male character – we don't know if Martin, with whom Roy and Joe meet for lunch – is straight or not. He is also, besides Roy, who is obviously unlikable, the play's only Republican with whom we are supposed to feel sympathy. Discussing the particular use of Mormons as representation for the conservative movement in America, Kushner explains that, as is the case with Judaism, in Mormonism there seems to be less abuse of patriarchal powers than in other conservative circles – abuse being defined by wife beating or incest, for example, not the general oppressive nature of patriarchy in Western culture. With Joe Kushner 'wanted to write a conservative man that I actually liked' however, he says 'I didn't finally succeed' (Savran, 1996: 311). Kushner's desire to write a likeable character is telling for the ambivalence towards him in the play. Joe is not a bad person as such. He wants to do what is best for Harper, but ultimately fails to do so. Where Harper had the bad luck of falling terribly in love with a man who couldn't love her, Joe has the bad luck of being gay in a culture that cannot accept his sexuality and this is where Mormonism, Reagan Republicanism and American power collide. Joe's attraction to Louis is initially painful as he struggles between doing what he has been taught is right and what he desires. His desire for Louis, and his acting on that desire, is a transgression that he does not know how to handle the consequences of within the religious and conservative paradigm of his thinking.

In an attempt to explain Joe's background, Kushner uses a Freudian model for explanation: part of the reason for Joe's sexuality is to be found in his complicated childhood relationship with his father. Joe's father was a military man who could be brutal and hard and Joe's initial admiration for the hardboiled Roy and their relationship as such can be read in relation to this Freudian model.

Roy Cohn

Though the character of Roy Cohn is based on the historical figure of Roy Cohn he is clearly a fictional construction by Kushner. Certain elements of Roy Cohn's history: his work for McCarthy, his work on the case against Ethel and Julius Rosenberg, his closeted homosexuality, his homophobia and his death of AIDS are all historical facts. Nevertheless, it is important to look at the character of Roy Cohn within the logic of the play itself. In the play, Roy Cohn functions as a link to, or the embodiment of, what Kushner sees as the corrupted power structure of America. Roy Cohn is the character who ensures that the essentially domestic scenes and struggles between Louis and Prior and Harper and Joe will be read through a larger socio-economic frame of American society, catastrophe and political history. We have seen earlier how Roy Cohn serves a central function in the play in creating the parallel between McCarthyism and Republicanism. He also functions, however, as a dramatic motor by nature of his relationship with Joe Pitt. The relationship between

Joe and Roy is a father/son relationship with clear sado-masochistic qualities, which lets Kushner point to the homo-erotic nature of most male relationships when it comes to issues of power. Roy's masculinity is completely tied up with the masculinity often equalled, at least for him, with power, which is why Roy, as a character, refuses to admit his homosexuality. Gay men, for the character Roy Cohn, are without any sort of political influence or importance so for him sex with men is an action and not something that defines his life. Being in power defines his life, which is ultimately why he tries to make Joe go to Washington as his protégé. Seeing gay men around him be marginalized and discriminated against, Roy Cohn refuses to accept an identity based on his sexual actions.

Michael Cadden has characterized Roy Cohn's function in the play: 'Cohn acts as the Satanic catalyst of the piece, forcing crises of identity and identification in many of the men who surround him' (Cadden, 1997: 84). While this is obviously true Cohn also serves as the embodiment of the Reagan era's and by extension Cold War America's interpretation and reliance on a certain creed of straight masculinity. He is an illustration of the Reagan era's fascination with the strong, individual, loner, which is also why Cohn cannot let himself be defined as a gay man since, according to him, the gay community has no power and without power there would be no Roy Cohn. It is here that AIDS intervenes and finally forces Roy Cohn into a community that he had battled tooth and nail, and this is the great irony of the play: Roy Cohn is accepted into a gay community that he has rejected by a black nurse who is a former drag queen. In the end Roy Cohn's nightmare becomes his final destination.

Belize

Belize is the only character of whom we know very, very, little in terms of background. We might know that the nurse Emily has a mother who embroiders and that this is driving Emily crazy, which is basically more than we know of Belize. Belize's male name is

Norman Ariaga and he is the only man in the play who is addressed
by a female name. He occasionally uses female forms in conversation
with Prior, but he is the only male character consistently addressed
by a female name. In a conversation between Prior and Belize full
of campy references, Belize says 'All this girl-talk shit is politically
incorrect, you know. We should have stopped it back when we gave
up a drag' (67). Belize is a reference to an earlier strategy of gay liberation and his continued use of that name marks him as part of the
historic struggle, and as part of that collective movement. His name
carries a relation to the community that he qua his nursing of the
dying exists within as the only character in the play. In an interview
with Bruce McLeod, Kushner addressed Belize as a character and
his function in the play. He said:

> I wanted him to be the ideological counterweight to Roy, that
> there were two people in the play who were not lost and inert
> and swimming around deeply confused. I wanted there to be
> two people, one of the Left and one of the Right, who had a very
> clear moral compass and knew exactly where they were in the uni-
> verse at all times, and who were not in theoretical, ethical crises.
> (McLeod, 1998: 80)

Read in this way Belize in a certain way becomes ground zero in
terms of the play's investigation of morals, ethics and politics during
a catastrophe. David Savran and David Román point to this construction of Belize as the only (living) character whose morals are
never questioned (Savran, 1997: 30). Belize then becomes, as drag
queens often do in popular culture, a sort of compassionate truth
teller marked as the ultimate outsider who has absolutely no way of
passing (unlike, for example, Louis, who 'butches up' for his family).

Hannah Pitt/Ethel Rosenberg
Hannah Porter Pitt and Ethel Rosenberg both play supporting parts
in the play and both are seemingly at the periphery of the play.

However, they both serve crucial roles in the plays' staging of the process of forgiveness, or perhaps, rather acceptance. Hannah Porter Pitt is on the surface a hard Mormon woman, who, at the play's beginning, knows exactly what is right and what is wrong. She exists within the dogma of her religion, though we see cracks in the plaster as soon as Joe calls and tells her he is gay. She immediately sells her house and takes off for New York. Though we get the sense that her religion is truly important to her, we also get the sense that Utah and Salt Lake City have become stifling to her. When her real-estate agent urges her to 'stay put', not unlike the reactionary angels do to Prior, Hannah expresses her exhaustion with Salt Lake City, its energy and lack of intelligence, so she sets out on her journey to New York City and her transformation. By her orgasm, induced by the erotic encounter with the Angel, Hannah becomes transformed into herself. Unlike Harper, who we never see as sexually fulfilled, Hannah's personality changes once the Angel breathes life into it. The same actress who plays Hannah Pitt also plays Ethel Rosenberg. Like Roy Cohn, Ethel Rosenberg is a historical character. Ethel Rosenberg was prosecuted along with her husband Julius Rosenberg for spying on behalf of the Soviet Union in connection with the atomic bomb. The case has sparked controversy among scholars ever since, debating whether or not the Rosenbergs were guilty spies or victims of an overzealous justice department eager to make a case. Post-Cold War scholarship seems to indicate that Julius Rosenberg probably had some guilt while Ethel Rosenberg probably was innocent. In any case, as with Roy Cohn, this is a fictional Ethel Rosenberg, who as a ghost pays a visit to the man who had her executed. Considering that Ethel and Hannah are played by the same character it proves interesting to look at both as mother figures, arriving, as the mother so often does in the theatre, to sort things out one last time. In her article on the play's representation of Jewish identity, Alisa Solomon presents a complicated reading of the Jewish characters and points to the complex part Ethel Rosenberg plays, saying that compared to the other characters 'Ethel occupies a third, more discomforting spot – indeed one that questions some of the core principles of capitalist America itself' (Solomon, 1997: 129). Solomon points out that Ethel Rosenberg serves as a connection between the two funerals of the prologues; that of Sarah Ironson and those like her, and that of Communism, since she is both the immigrant and the Communist. This, naturally, complicates her role as a mother. Hannah does not forgive; neither does Ethel. Ethel Rosenberg makes it clear that she has come to see Roy Cohn suffer and die. Yet, once he is actually dead she, like Belize, takes pity on him (Belize because he is gay, Ethel because he is Jewish – essentially equating gayness with ethnicity) and helps Louis say the Kaddish over him.

The Angel

The Angel is a crucial character in the play. Though the play has other otherworldly beings, namely the ghosts, the Angel carries special significance in the way she combines the real and fantastic, the earthbound and cosmological in the play. She, along with the other apparitions to a lesser degree, is the messenger of catastrophe that Prior must overcome to make the world keep spinning forward. She is not the angel Moroni who appeared to Joseph Smith and showed him the Golden Tablets on which Mormonism is founded, and she is not Walter Benjamin's male angel either. She is clearly marked as the Angel of America; Kushner describes her as 'Four divine emanations, Flour, Phosphor, Lumen, and Candle; manifest in One: the Continental Principality of America. She has magnificent steel-gray wings' (9). The other angels, or Continental Principalities, as Kushner describes them, represent the different parts of the world. They are all 'inconceivably powerful Celestial Apparatcik/ Bueraucrat-Angels' (138). It follows from this that the angels in the theology of *Angels in America*, though constructed primarily from Mormon and Jewish influences, are magnificent yet powerless, and essential to the logic of the play: neither Mormon nor Jewish, but a quite American combination of the two. Since God has left the angels and heaven they are roaming around aimlessly, unable to take control since they can only administer not instigate action. The Angel that crashes through Prior's ceiling can be read within these binaries; powerful/weak, heavenly/earthly (after all she pulls a muscle in her thigh wrestling with Prior), male/female. However, Kushner's ultimate deconstruction of how we are used to thinking about angels is that she is, and by extension all the angels are, wrong. Prior proves the angels wrong by declining to accept their reactionary agenda to stop the world from moving forward. In an article in the *New York Times* about Ellen McLaughlin, who played the Angel in all the early American productions of the play, Kushner talks about the Angel describing how her lines are very difficult in that the 'writing teeters between almost parody and very, very dense, I don't know, mumbo jumbo almost incomprehensible language'. But, he continues, 'What straddles that in Ellen's performance is this tower-ing fury' (Weber, 1994b). This indicates the extent to which we have to consider this angel not just in relation to the Mormon or Jewish tradition for angels, but really, rather, look at her within the logic of the play itself. This is a furious, tired, and somewhat broken down angel.

Influences, genre and style

Keeping in mind Christopher Bigsby's image of Kushner as a man walking through a snowstorm of influences, it is obvious that *Angels in America* draws on multiple layers of inspiration and influences. This section seeks to outline some of them and discuss the element of genre.

If there is one iconic image from *Angels in America* it is the spec-tacular angel crashing through an AIDS infected gay man's bedroom ceiling in the middle of the 1980s. The Angel hovering about his bed, proclaiming that 'the great work begins', has graced posters and book covers. This is the central image that connects the two plays, repeated as it is in *Perestroika*. The image represents the opening that cracks history wide open, as Ethel Rosenberg predicts it will before the ambulance carries Roy Cohn off to the hospital and, eventually, his death.

The inspiration for this angel is taken from Walter Benjamin's (1892–1940) 'Theses on the Philosophy of History' in which he describes a painting by Paul Klee called 'Angelus Novus' portraying an angel blowing backwards through space while staring back at where he came from. The angel faces the past, which we might perceive as a chain of events, but he sees it as one large catastrophe. Yet he is constantly blown forwards by a storm from paradise while debris from the past piles up around his feet. In Benjamin's description the storm from paradise:

> has gotten caught in his wings with such violence that the angel can no longer close them. The storm irresistibly propels him into the future to which his back is turned, while the pile of debris before him grows skyward. This storm is what we call progress. (Benjamin, 1968: 257–258)

Though the angel in *Angels in America* is female (or rather 'hermaphroditically Equipped as well with a Bouquet of Phalli' (175)) it is clearly the same angel who wishes for Prior to stop the wind, the catastrophe, and finally let the world rest and no longer move forward. The use of Benjamin's angel is more than just spectacular, it lends the play its governing philosophy: that change is absolutely essential though painful, and that it is necessary to remember history to envision a future. That human existence is dialectically constructed between the past and the future.

Following Kushner's belief in the importance of history it is necessary to look at *Angels in America* in relation to the contemporary theatre in the 1980s and early 1990s and in relation to the representation of gay men on stage in general. The theatrical representation of gay male sexuality basically followed two trends beginning in the late 1960s: mainstream productions such as Mart Crowley's *The Boys in the Band* (1968), Martin Sherman's *Bent* (1979) and Harvey Fierstein's *Torch Song Trilogy* (Broadway 1982), and more underground theatrical productions such as Charles Ludlam's Ridiculous Theatrical Company in the East Village in New York City. The mainstream plays broke down barriers by the way they gave visibility to the existence of gay men on stage and in society while the less mainstream plays offered new modes of production of a certain gay sensibility, a certain gay style, a certain way of seeing the world that Kushner acknowledges as important for his own writing. *Angels in America* shares obvious elements with all three mainstream plays. It shares a certain Jewish and Camp humour and sensibility with *The Boys in the Band* without adopting its self-hating characters (though Louis at times displays a certain element of self-loathing that could be taken out of Crowley's play). The difference, however, is that Louis does not loathe his sexuality but his actions, while with Crowley's characters it is the other way around. *Angels in America* shares a notion of the importance of history with *Bent*, which stages the Nazi persecution of gay men during the Second World War. In *Bent* as in *Angels in America,* the audience is reminded that oppression of gay male sexuality is a historical phenomenon that must be understood as such in order to be challenged. It also shares a number of elements with *Torch Song Trilogy*. In *Torch Song Trilogy* the audience follows Arnold, a New York drag queen, in his struggles to find a man and establish a family. Through three acts – all performed in different styles, a monologue, a fugue and a realistic situation comedy – we follow Arnold's trials and tribulations culminating in a fight with his mother. As Alan Sinfield has pointed out, *Torch Song Trilogy* 'has split scenes, the discarded female partner, and mother flying in to sort things out' (Sinfield, 1999: 205). Despite their similarities

Angels in America is a very different gay-play (however stiff a category that is) than *Torch Song Trilogy* in terms of its politics. In *Torch Song Trilogy* Arnold only wants what his mother has. He wants her life – a house, man and child – while the characters in *Angels in America* have been radicalized by AIDS. The Utopian dream in *Angels in America* is not a dream of assimilation but rather a dream of equality and citizenship based in recognition and valuation of difference.

This radicalization of politics can also be seen in a radicalization of the theatrical form. For this Kushner acknowledges his debt to Charles Ludlam and his fabulous theatre. Charles Ludlam founded the Ridiculous Theatrical Company in 1967 (2 years before the Stonewall Riots) and, until his untimely death from AIDS in 1987, the company produced a series of plays, most in a fantastic, over-the-top, campy and ridiculous style and often in a non-logical form. Kushner sees Ludlam's theatre as a sort of first generation gay theatre and his own as a second generation. This generational transformation can be called the change from the ridiculous to the fabulous. What Kushner calls the theatre of the fabulous utilizes a notion of history (standing on the shoulders of the ridiculous) and politics. The politics of the fabulous, as it is inspiring Kushner, comes from a Queer Nation chant: 'We're here. We're Queer. We're Fabulous. Get used to it'. Fabulous in one sense evolves beyond ridiculous in the way that fabulous becomes a rejection of the weakness inherent in being stigmatized as ridiculous. Fabulous rejects being perceived as weak or suffering in relation to oppression. Another related sense is that this use of fabulous is a historical awareness of gay history and gay theatre history that Ludlam, at least the pre-Stonewall Ludlam, could not have (Cunningham, 1998: 62–76; Savran, 1996: 299–301). In Kushner's own relation to gay theatre history, then, we see the same dialectic between the past and the future that governs *Angel in America*. He is inspired by, and in conversation with, the writers who came before him: Tennessee Williams, Mart Crowley, Martin Sherman, Harvey Fierstein, Robert Patrick, Larry Kramer and William Hoffman but feels that he belongs to a group of new writers such as Holly Hughes, David Greenspan, Tim Miller and Paula Vogel (Cunningham, 1998: 69; Savran, 1996: 299).

Besides standing in relation to previous gay writers and the theatrical representations of gay men, the obvious inspiration for Kushner, as we saw in the biography, is Bertolt Brecht. In an interview with his mentor Carl Weber, who taught Kushner at NYU, Kushner remembers his first encounters with the theatre and theory of Bertolt Brecht. In a modern drama class he read Brecht's *Threepenny Opera* and *The Good Person from Sezuan* without being considerably impressed. However, after being presented with Ernst Fischer's theory of the artist's responsibility towards society, seeing Richard Foreman's production of *Threepenny Opera* several times, and reading Brecht's writing on the theatre in *Brecht on Theater,* he realized that Brecht had successfully suggested a way in which a committed public intellectual could work productively in the theatre. The intervention in history and society that Kushner intended to create with *Angels in America* then is ultimately as deeply indebted to the theories and practices of Brecht as it is to the narrative American dramatic tradition exemplified in Tennessee Williams's early plays.

Though the practices and theatre of Brecht have been widely debated and contested since his death, there is no doubt that his creation of 'epic theatre' changed the twentieth-century's theatre. Brecht's epic theatre is based in his Marxist political beliefs and his antipathy towards the theatre of his time – what he called a culinary theatre in which the audience was seduced to complete identification and therefore, presumably, asked no critical questions of the world it saw reproduced on stage. Brecht wanted an active political theatre that allowed, even demanded, its audience to ask questions and think critically about the fictional world on stage. However, and this is a common misinterpretation of Brecht's theatre, Brecht insisted that the theatre should always also be entertaining as he describes in *Short Organum for the Theatre* (Brecht, 1964: 180).

The theatre should teach, but it should do so in an entertaining way through songs, spectacles, and so forth. Kushner's favourite play by Brecht, *Mother Courage,* is a history play set during the Thirty Years War (1618–1648) in Europe. Through representing events as historical, Brecht creates the distance between the work and the spectator that he finds necessary to prevent the spectator from a complete, passive, identification. Through this treatment, he can make the spectator watch the play and not just say 'that's how I would act' but add 'if I had lived under those circumstances'. Through this process, an awareness of the social situation arises that can be used in the struggle for change. When producing contemporary works dealing with current issues, the events should be produced as if they were historical. If doing so, Brecht's theory goes, the spectator will find the actions odd which will, potentially, make the spectator reflect on his/her own actions in the contemporary world (Brecht, 1964: 190). Clearly, this is a technique Kushner applies in *Angels in America*, a history play dealing with very contemporary issues. In order to prevent the audience from a total identification with the character, Brecht invented what he called 'verfremdung': an acting (and directing) technique in which breaks were created through which the spectator would be reminded of the fictional nature of the theatrical event. These breaks could be an actor speaking directly to the audience, a song where the actor commented on his own character or the action of the play, a breakdown of the established fictional reality, songs, monologues and design elements pointing to themselves as such. Multiple times throughout *Angels in America* we find these Brechtian devices used. In Kushner's 'note about the staging' it says:

> The moments of magic – the appearance and disappearance of Mr. Lies and the ghosts, the Book hallucination, and the ending – are to be fully realized, as bits of wonderful *theatrical* illusion – which means it's OK if the wires show, and may be it's

good that they do, but the magic should at the same time be thoroughly amazing (p. 11).

Having the Angel's wires show points to the fact that the Angel is indeed, one, not real angel and, two, an actor suspended from a piece of stage machinery pretending to be an angel in a play by Tony Kushner. However, and we sense an ambiguity here, Kushner insists that this be amazing, which we can interpret as meaning entertaining just like Brecht would have wanted it. Brecht's influence in the theatre was much larger in Europe and particular in Great Britain following the tour of the Berliner Ensemble in 1956 than it has been in America, and Kushner is quite inspired by the way British playwrights have adopted a Brechtian dramaturgy and particularly as it can be seen in the writings of Caryl Churchill with plays such as *Vinegar Tom*, *Cloud Nine* and *Top Girls*.

Kushner subtitles his play 'A Gay Fantasia on National Themes'. Fantasia as a musical form has roots in improvisation and is a piece of music not adhering to any particular mode or form. It is centred in the composer's fancy or imagination. As a theatrical genre, this does not exist. Kushner breaks down the boundaries between particular genres (such as comedy, tragedy and tragicomedy) and mixes these in a 'fantastic' way. *Millennium Approaches* follows traditional theatrical forms closer than *Perestroika* with its increased moves between the real and the imagined, between earth and heaven, between the living and the dead. Both plays mix the comical with the tragic, the domestic with the public or political, and the real with the imagined. The plays have characteristics of expressionistic plays such as August Strindberg's *A Dream Play* along with elements of medieval theatre such as the simultaneity and the abundance of religious symbols. The genre of *Angels in America*, however, is probably closest to that of the history play as outlined by Brecht before. It is the investigation of recent history that connects all the disparate elements in the play. Kushner says about the relationship between

the theatre and history that 'Americans suffer from collective
Amnesia; our own past is lost to us. Theater has always had a vital
relationship to history; the examination and, yes, the *teaching* of
history has to be accounted a function of any political theater'
(Kushner, 1997: 28). Through his use of an eclectic mix of theatrical genres and Brechtian devices Kushner then lives up to Walter
Benjamin's description of a historical materialist, whom Benjamin
describes as one who 'regards it as his task to brush history against
the grain' (Benjamin, 1968: 257).

Close readings of key scenes

Millennium Approaches, act 1, scene 1

Perestroika, act 1, scene 1 and epilogue

The first scene of each play functions as a prologue to the play
despite not being named so. Structurally the two opening scenes
lead us into the play and construct a frame through which to understand the actions, the breakdown of order and finally, perhaps, the
possibility for change.

It is significant that *Millennium Approaches* opens with a funeral;
something has died and disappeared and the survivors are left to
make order of what remains. Though this is the funeral of an individual, Sarah Ironson, grandmother of Louis, the Rabbi makes clear
that it is also the end of an era. Likening her, in a joke, to one of the
last Native Americans the Rabbi creates a parallel between the disappearance of the Jewish people who migrated to the USA from
Eastern Europe, settled in the Bronx or in Brooklyn, and the eras-
ure of the Native Americans as a people. In this parallel we find a
notion of tribal belonging which governs the structures of experience of its members. This order has disappeared forever with Sarah
Ironson. The Rabbi describes how Sarah Ironson and her fellow
immigrants left Lithuania and Russia for America and how they

fought for the Jewish home in New York, in America, so their children 'would not grow up here, in this strange place, in the melting pot where nothing melted' and he continues 'You do not live in America, no such place exists' (16), suggesting instead that their identity is fundamentally constructed by the country and culture that the predecessors left. In this sweeping denial of America as a category, as a unity and as an identity lies a fundamental premise that the play sets out to investigate. Does America exist and, if so, what constitutes it? Along with questioning America and, by extension, the impossibility of being an American (in the melting pot where nothing melted) the Rabbi expresses that although Sarah Ironson's journey lives within each and every one of her children and grandchildren, it is no longer possible to take the journey from the old world to the new world. '[S]uch Great Voyages do not anymore exist' (16) the rabbi claims, but the play ultimately ends up negating that. Such journeys do indeed exist. Louis and Prior are on a journey, Joe Pitt is on a journey from being closeted to being out, and Hanna Pitt is on her way to becoming a fuller more understanding person. Harper, of course, is last seen floating somewhere close to the Ozone layer on her overnight flight to San Francisco – literally on a journey (after all her imaginary friend is a travel agent). Their journey is perhaps no longer that of the Jewish immigrant, who came from Lithuania to Grand Concourse Avenue in the Bronx, or to Flatbush in Brooklyn, or that of the Mormon believer migrating across the plains to Utah, but it is a journey for that Jewish woman's children and their grandchildren and their children again. That journey, if we accept the hope of the epilogue, is a constant journey into becoming, not into being, American.

The opening scene of *Perestroika* is set in the Kremlin, the seat of the governing body in the Soviet Union in Moscow, where the world's oldest Bolshevik, Aleksii Antedilluvianovich Prelapsarianov, is addressing his party in front of a large red flag. The old Bolshevik, the description indicating that he was part of the original Russian Revolution and the movement that later became the Communist Party of the Soviet Union, is addressing the notion of change. In reference to classical tradition the Bolshevik is blind, like all seers such as Cassandra and Teiresias from classic Greek tragedy. Taking place in January of 1986, this was a time of great change taking place within the Soviet Union due to Gorbachev, then General Secretary of the Communist Party in the Soviet Union, and his process of economic restructuring in the Soviet Union begun in the summer of 1985. Defining Perestroika as a revolution and a 'decisive acceleration of the socio-economic and cultural development of society which involves radical changes on the way to a qualitatively new state', Gorbachev undertook the enormous project in an attempt to save Communism (Gorbachev, 1987: 50). The old Bolshevik is directly addressing this radical attempt to change. Just as the Rabbi formulated the notions of history, identity and journey in his eulogy for Sarah Ironson, the Bolshevik formulates the fundamental questions that structure *Perestroika*. He asks, 'The Great Question before us is: Are we doomed? The Great Question before us is: Will the Past release us? The Great Question before us is: Can we Change? In Time?' (147). He does not give the answers to his questions but warns the Party (and by extension the audience who, as he says, 'Live in this Sour little Age' (148)) that though change is absolutely necessary it must be based upon a theory as bold as the original theory, Marxism. However no such theory is to be found and the Bolshevik laments the overtaking of his theory by market incentives, American cheeseburgers and watered-down Bukharinite stopgap makeshift Capitalism (148).

Where the Rabbi's opening monologue is a funeral for an individual, this is a funeral for a system. Through the words of the blind Bolshevik we attend the funeral of the Soviet Union: the funeral of the dream, or what Prelapsarianov calls the beautiful theory, Marxism. This, the second prologue, bemoaning the collapse of Marxism, is systemic. Where the first prologue complicated the notion of the possibility of a singular America and a singular American identity the second one concerns the ideological systems under which we live and, by consequence, these systems or world orders falling apart without any obvious replacements. Like the angels roaming around in the heaven that God abandoned, we are left drifting in the shifting ideological wind from paradise.

If the two opening scenes introduce the audience to the central themes and questions of the plays, the epilogue closes and concludes by opening up the play to the future (Kushner had initially planned several more plays about the characters). It is the closing frame and combines issues of the individual or personal with issues of the systemic or the public. Again, in the epilogue, the personal becomes political. Louis, Belize, Hannah and Prior sit in front of the Bethesda Fountain in Central Park, New York City, on a cold February day in 1999, 4 years after the end of *Perestroika*. Prior is, obviously, still alive and Hannah is 'noticeably different – she looks like a New Yorker, and is reading the *New York Times*' (277). The transformed characters have entered a new decade and a transformed world. It is the early 1990s, when Reagan is gone, the Berlin Wall has fallen, the Soviet Union is clearly about to collapse, and the established order of the Cold War has been overthrown, blown away like dried leaves in the first fall storm. The possibility for change suddenly seems real. Prior, the play's unwilling prophet, gets the last word. While Louis and Belize discuss the situation between Israel and Palestine, Prior turns to the audience and says:

This disease will be the end of many of us, but not nearly all, and the dead will be commemorated and will struggle on with the living, and we are not going away. We won't die secret deaths anymore. The world only spins forward. We will be citizens. The Time has come. Bye now.

You are fabulous creatures, each and every one.

And I bless you: More Life.
The Great Work Begins. (280)

This progress-will-make-us-citizens-despite-suffering-and-death epilogue is central to the play by the light it sheds backwards on the hours of theatrical rhetoric we, as audiences, have moved through in forward motion. The epilogue serves as a political commentary on the individual actions performed by the characters throughout the performance and the transformation these actions lead to in the intertwined lives of the characters. It applies the critique of Reaganism and its consequences presented in the play to society as such and not just to the individual. In doing so the epilogue structurally mirrors the function of the two prologues.

Millennium Approaches, **act 1, scene 7**
Perestroika, **act 3, scene 3**

Several times throughout the play Harper and Prior are connected in somewhat unusual situations; either in hallucinations or, as at the Mormon Visitors Center, in a situation that breaks down the barrier between the real and the imagined. Connecting Prior and Harper in this way indicates that both are able to see something besides the given reality in which Louis and Joe exist. They are given certain powers that allow them to gain insight into what is happening to the world around them though, most times, it does not allow them to handle their own private situation in a better way.

The first time Prior and Harper meet each other Prior is having a dream and Harper is in a Valium-induced hallucination. As the scene opens, Prior is in front of a magnificent make-up table in the process of applying drag make-up. Obviously this is a representation of Prior as he used to be before he stopped doing drag, before he got sick, and in some ways, before the world went astray. The fact that both Belize and Prior have stopped doing drag is a comment on the development, or lack of, the gay liberation movement. Drag as a form relates to the form of the ridiculous and turned out to be a strategy that did not necessarily work. By letting Prior put on his make-up and quote the gay classic *Sunset Boulevard* with 'I'm ready for my close-up Mr. Demille', Kushner establishes Prior as a character at a point in between the past and the present. He says:

One wants to move through life with elegance and grace, blossoming infrequently but with exquisite taste, and perfect timing, like a rare bloom, a zebra orchid . . . One wants... But one so seldom gets what one wants, does one? No. One does not. One gets fucked. Over. One . . . dies at thirty, robbed of . . . decades of majesty. (36)

In this speech we follow a transformation from the past – the wish to be a rare bloom, a zebra orchid – to the present where AIDS has changed everything, killing off not only a particular group of citizens, but a whole way of life. Like Norma Desmond, the main character in *Sunset Boulevard*, who is a silent movie star whose art has become obsolete because of the advance of talkies, Prior's drag is no longer sufficient to explain his life. As he says 'Oh my queen; you know you've hit rock-bottom when even drag is a drag' (37). At this intersection, 'the threshold of revelation' (39) as they call it later, the threshold between past, present and future, Harper arrives into Prior's dream to great confusion for both of them. After getting acquainted, finding out that Harper is Mormon and Prior gay, Harper leaps into theorizing about the limits of imagination, saying 'Imagination can't create anything new, can it? It only recycles bits and pieces from the world and reassembles them into visions' and she continues 'Nothing unknown is knowable' (37). Besides providing insight into the character of Harper; her unhappiness, her reliance on Valium to take her away from the 'unbearable ordinariness and, well, untruthfulness of our lives' (37) the discussion concerning the relationship between the past and our ability to imagine a future is central to the play's constant underlying dialectic between the past and the present. Can we really imagine change if we don't understand the history of oppression? – the play seems to ask. Both characters, but particularly Harper, carry this theme throughout the two plays as a connecting force. Being at the threshold of revelation, as they are, Harper sees that Prior is sick, but declares that deep inside part of him remains uninfected. Prior on the other hand declares Joe, Harper's husband, to be 'a homo'. Their meeting in Valium-dreamland sets their individual lives in motion – both will be left fairly soon because of the truths revealed to them in this scene – but also introduces the visions that Prior is about to receive at the end of the scene as fundamentally connected to the past. Though he must learn to reject the angel he already knows, deep inside, the answer is 'Nothing unknown is knowable' (38).

In *Perestroika*, act 3 scene 3, Harper and Prior share another scene that parallels the hallucination scene from *Millennium Approaches*. After Joe has left her, Harper is being taken care of by Hannah who brings her to the Mormon Visitors Center where Hannah works, and Harper sits in the Diorama Room. Prior, claiming to be doing research on angels, following his visitation, shows up and the two recognize each other from the threshold of revelation. He is there to see the diorama of a Mormon family crossing the plains on their way to Utah. This is the scene that most clearly references Mormonism as a religion, showing its function as an example of migration and fundamental American religion within the play.

The diorama that Harper and Prior are watching specifically foregrounds the migrant experience of the Mormons as they ventured West to settle and create a Mormon kingdom. As used in the play, the diorama connects Joe and Harper's Mormon roots with those of Louis's Jewish Grandmother, and Prior's WASPY family in New England. Of these tales of migration however, the Mormon one ranks alone in its specific American nature. Mormonism is both in and of America and thus represents a specific American experience.

Not unlike the reactionary angels, the Mormons, sought refuge from the pluralism – religious and political – of early nineteenth-century America. The migration West can be seen as much as a flight from something as a journey towards something (Mauss, 1994: 24). As the two met in their first hallucination and shared initial insights into each other's lives they meet again here to further their own migration towards their individual, yet shared, progress.

Millennium Approaches, act 1, scene 9

The last scene of the first act, throughout which we have been introduced to the central characters, their tribulations and the main themes of the play, constitutes the outing of Roy Cohn; the Cold-War lawyer who participated in the prosecution of Julius and Ethel Rosenberg, the life-long Republican, and the closeted homosexual. In his insightful article 'Strange Angel: The Pinklisting of Roy Cohn', Michael Cadden investigates the essentially homophobic reaction to the death of Roy Cohn in both the mainstream and the gay press, and reads this as a 'pinklisting', playing, obviously, with the activity of blacklisting that Roy Cohn and Joseph McCarthy were engaged in during the 1950s. However, Cadden points out, Kushner takes a more nuanced approach to Roy Cohn placing 'Cohn at the center of his examination of gay identity and community' working from the 'assumption that Cohn's identity, and gay identity in general, is at the center of contemporary American life' (Cadden, 1997: 83). Kushner, then, may 'out' Roy Cohn in this scene, but he does not necessarily pinklist him. Criticism of the performances has shown that one of the most interesting elements in Kushner's portrait of Cohn is the strange sympathy the character, though thoroughly unlikeable, wins from an audience.

As the scene opens Cohn has come to see his doctor, Henry, who explains the virus and its consequences in scientific terms. We have already learned that Prior is sick and we are now introduced to the second AIDS character. Together they form a complete set of opposites. Though we later see Prior go through medical check-ups, Roy Cohn is the man with AIDS who is clearly pathologized in this scene through the medical discourse used to discuss his disease. Following the diagnosis, Roy asks why he is being told all this about a disease that 'afflicts mostly gay men and drug addicts' (49) since he is not gay. While challenging Henry to say that Roy Cohn is gay, Cohn also threatens to destroy his career if he does so. Without mentioning the word 'gay' Henry says to Roy that he has had sex with 'men many many times' and that 'one of them or any number of them, has made you very sick. You have AIDS' (51). The discussion that follows illustrates in crucial ways Roy's theory of sexuality, power and identity. Rejecting the idea that who you sleep with identifies who you are, accusing Henry of being too 'hung up on words, on labels' (51), Cohn lays forth his own theory of identity:

> No. Like all labels they tell you one thing and one thing only: where does an individual so identified fit in the food chain, in the pecking order? Not ideology, or sexual taste, but something much simpler: clout. Not who I fuck or who fucks me, but who will pick up the phone when I call, who owes me favors. (51)

Here we see Roy Cohn's central split between power and sexuality leading to his ultimate rejection of a movement based on identity politics. Roy Cohn could never identify himself as a gay man because according to him 'Homosexuals are men who know nobody and who nobody knows. Who have zero clout' (51). Roy Cohn in the scene then positions himself as the ultimate 'other' in relation to Prior/Louis/Belize who are the out-and-proud gay liberals of the play. In Cohn's statements following what is essentially his death sentence, Cohn insists to be dying of liver cancer in order to not die a gay man – AIDS, at least at the time, being a 'gay disease'. Because of his power and the way this power constitutes his masculinity, Roy Cohn, the character, could function within the paradigm of

Cold War American culture as a very powerful man. He, as he says towards the end of the scene, could bring his lover to the White House and shake hands with President Reagan 'Because what I am is defined entirely by who I am. Roy Cohn is not a homosexual. Roy Cohn is a heterosexual man, Henry, who fucks around with guys' (52). Cohn's perceived split between action and identity is ultimately proven to be false since not all the power in the world could save him from dying of AIDS, though he gets his hands on the coveted medicine. The civil disobedience, or let's call it activism, performed by Louis and Belize in the end when stealing the medicine after Roy's death then becomes an ironic end to Roy's life. By using his power to get the medicine he ends up helping a community to which he had no intention of belonging. Through the character of Belize, during the scenes in *Perestroika* taking place in Roy's hospital room, the gay community, symbolized with the most flamboyant gay man in the play, claims Roy. He ends up consumed by his own sexuality.

Changing views of the play

In his seminal essay on the play, David Savran states that 'The opposite of nearly everything you say about *Angels in America* will also hold true' which is a fundamental premise in his reading of the play's thematic and political ambiguity, an ambiguity that I believe has driven the writings on the plays from its first production until today. (Savran, 1997: 14). It is also, however, a statement that one should keep in mind when thinking about the changing interpretations of the play and its meaning(s). In the 15 years since its original productions much has been said and written about *Angels in America*. The criticism stretches from reviews, profiles, portraits, interviews in newspapers, to scholarly treatments of the play, discussing its themes and politics, its merits and failures. *Angels in America* is a complicated play and the discourse surrounding it matches it fully.

The initial critical response to *Angels in America* was predominantly positive – except for Conservative or right-wing newspapers who disagreed with the play's bleak portrait of Reagan's America. In the so-called more liberal press, the *New York Times* had numerous articles about Tony Kushner and the play including reviews of the different productions. Frank Rich, then the lead critic, wrote an article meditating on what he claimed was a needed 'transition from an old Broadway to a new one' claiming that Tony Kushner and *Angels in America* was part of the solution to this. The theatrical landscape in which *Angels in America* was performed was one of great stagnation, according to Rich, who warns that if Broadway is to survive 'There is no time to waste'. In Rich's article *Angels in America* comes to the rescue and presents Kushner as a playwright whose work is:

> nothing less than a radical vision of American society, politics, and religion, as written in the uncompromisingly extravagant voice of a homosexual leftist intellectual who will try anything (except conventional social realism) to turn original ideas and life-and-death emotions into gripping and often ferociously funny theater. (Rich, 1993a)

Rich expresses hope that *Angels in America* can bring a new audience to Broadway and take American playwriting out of its domestic realm and into the political world. He creates a dichotomy between the past and the present that the play wouldn't necessarily agree with, though he also does seem to say that *Angels in America* was the right play for the right time. Most of the criticism written about *Angels in America*, and David Román points this out as well, is written after the 1992 American presidential elections in which Bill Clinton defeated George H. W. Bush and ended 12 years of Republican rule in the White House. Roman points to the way that this change in power highlighted the play's function as a history play since it truly did analyse something that was now over, that is, in the past (Román, 1998: 205–224). In the first hopeful days of the Clinton presidency, *Angels in America* became somehow translated into a new time. Keeping in mind that Rich had earlier called *Millennium Approaches* 'Miraculous' it seemed as if both the theatre and its surrounding society suddenly had the ability to change. It seemed almost like a Benjaminian moment where 'history burst wide open' allowing for at least a spectre of change. Rich points this out when writing:

> What has really affected 'Angels in America' during the months of its odyssey to New York, however, is not so much its change of directors as Washington's change of Administrations. When first seen a year or so ago, the play seemed defined by its anger at the reigning political establishment, which tended to reward the Roy Cohns and ignore the Prior Walters. Mr. Kushner has not revised the text since – a crony of Cohns still boasts the Republican lock on the White House till year 2000 – but the shift in Washington has had the subliminal effect of making 'Angels in America' seem more focused on what happens next than on the past. (Rich, 1993b)

What Rich points out here, without ever saying it directly, is the play's Brechtian device. That it historicizes the recent, almost present, past to comment on the present and point to the future. David Richards, also writing in the *New York Times*, makes the same observation but somewhat differently. In a review of *Perestroika* he first claims that in *Millennium Approaches*, Kushner demonstrated virtues such as 'an intrepid theatricality, stinging intellect, and an engaging proclivity for undercutting himself with humor' and that these virtues are even greater in *Perestroika*, which he sees as a better and, ultimately, much more hopeful play than the brooding *Millennium Approaches*. The hope that Richards sees produced by the play, however, comes only at the very end of the play since most of the characters are actually worse off initially. In the end, in Richards's interpretation, Kushner speaks directly to the audience when Prior tells us that:

> Mankind will save itself. Or no one will. That is the daunting reality of Mr. Kushner's huge drama and also its humane promise. The choice is ours. 'The great work begins,' says Prior as the curtain falls. He's looking right at us. (Richards, 1993)

The reviews cited above represent only a fraction of the reviews written about the play and its productions worldwide (in the performance history section of this book I look more closely at some international reviews) but they represent an elated, very positive, trend in the initial reception of the plays.

To date there are two anthologies specifically on the play: *Angels in America: Essays on Kushner's Angels* (1995) and *Approaching the Millennium: Essays on Angels in America* (1997). The academic interest in the play and in Tony Kushner's writings in general clearly matches that of the initial newspaper criticism. The number of journal articles, book chapters, essays, and so forth grows every year and *Angels in America* seems to continue to garner interest. Obviously this has to do with the amount of information, references, intellectual material and theatrical qualities of the play. Though basically all of the essays and articles commend the plays for the same reasons that the newspaper criticism did, most of the analyses put forth in these volumes also put forth certain criticisms, two of which will be presented here.

David Savran analyses the inherent political ambivalence in the play. A quote from his article opened this section saying that because of the play's scope and politics anything you say about the play the opposite can also be true. Savran shows us that *Angels in America* envisions Utopia and dystopia as inherently connected, meaning that disaster is necessary in order to imagine Utopia which is why everybody, except Roy Cohn who dies, must look disaster in the eye before moving on. Building on this fundamental dichotomy, Utopia/dystopia, the play is structured around a series of other dichotomies such as: heaven/hell, forgiveness/retribution, communitarianism/individualism, spirit/flesh, pleasure/pain, beauty/decay, future/past, homosexuality/heterosexuality, rationalism/indeterminacy, migration/staying put, progress/stasis, life/death (Savran, 1997: 18). These dichotomies should not just be read as binary ends against which the characters and themes are played out, but rather, Savran suggests, as figures of undecidability. It is in the contradiction between them that meaning lies and not, as we would usually think, in the resolution of the conflict between them. Read in this way the contradictions in the play, and in and between the characters, are representations of struggle and in that struggle progress itself is thematized. Savran also makes clear that it seems like Kushner's politics, and thereby the play, favours communitarianism, rationalism and progress over their counterparts. However, despite its seemingly progressive nature and intent, it is questionable if the play's undecidability prevents a true political stance from being taken. If everybody can read the play exactly how they please, then, ultimately, what is the progressive message that so much initial newspaper criticism seemed to find buried under the represented rubble of a crumbling nation? How can a play giving such a scathing criticism of American society become such a success unless the audience, and the system of production in which it is mounted, can read something redeeming into it?

While basically agreeing with David Savran, Janelle Reinelt offers a slightly different view in her criticism of *Angels in America* as epic theatre. Concisely outlining the history (or rather lack thereof) of Brechtian epic theatre in America, Reinelt reads Kushner in relation to Brecht, his professed predecessor. Finding many redeeming qualities, like Savran, in the play, Reinelt ultimately ends up pointing out how the play displaces the essential Marxist notion of class onto questions of every other sort of identity (Reinelt, 1997: 242). Though we meet characters of varying religious, sexual and racial markers none of the main characters exist outside the middle class – the ghosts excepted. We get the sense that Roy Cohn belongs to an upper-class, but more because of his power than his financial abilities, of which we hear little besides the fact that he has embezzled some clients and, partly therefore, is being disbarred. The only poor person we encounter is in fact a psychotic homeless woman in the South Bronx, who is mostly in the play for comic relief. The only group for which we are not given a chance to feel sympathy is the poor, or the working class. This abandonment of class strikes Reinelt as strange for a professed socialist playwright as it consequentially leads to a renewed focus on the bourgeois individual. Though *Angels in America* strives hard to work with a collective subject, a group of people rather than the tribulations of one particular character, it ultimately ends up focusing on the individual. It is Prior's individual rejection of stasis that drives the play, and by extension, the world forward. Reinelt also offers us an example of the reinscribed individualism by reading the scene in which Belize strong-arms some bottles of AZT, by winning an abusive and racist argument with Roy Cohn. Belize, after getting the medicine from Cohn, admits to him that she needs them for some friends, and this is where individualism takes over on behalf of the possibility for a collective movement. By only framing Belize's actions in relation to Prior and not a community as such, Belize's activism ends up reifying individualism rather than being an example of a potential collective struggle. Both Reinelt and Savran in their analysis read if not history, then Kushner, against the grain, concluding that despite the play's many qualities as theatre it ends up somewhat short as political theatre. The abundance of theories and influences creates multiple cracks in the American hegemony, no doubt about that.

Cracks where an audience member might for a moment burst history open and start anew. However, in the end, the play in all its grandeur leads us back to us, its initial audience at least, individuals in America.

3 Production History

This chapter offers a brief history of American and international productions of *Angels in America*. It looks at the complicated process of the initial three American productions and the 1992 British production. Following that it looks at some international productions of the play, and the HBO TV version of the play. The history of a dramatic work needs to include the history of its scenic productions, as it is in the transformation from text to stage that a play becomes a performance and eventually takes on the form in which it will meet its audience.

Initial American productions

Kushner has repeatedly acknowledged the importance and contributions of a number of people to the writing of *Angels in America*. Numerous dramaturges, actors and directors have worked on the two plays, given suggestions for scenes, cuts, character developments, and so forth. Though the complete work is obviously Tony Kushner's, it is important to realize that theatre is a collaborative art and that a play can change drastically in the hands of different directors, designers and actors. This chapter can only introduce a fraction of the many talented artists worldwide who have worked on *Angels in America*. It outlines the play's quite complicated creation process by highlighting the initial productions in Los Angeles, San Francisco, New York and the 1992 London production, which put *Angels in America* on the international theatrical map. This performance history also illustrates the American production system of readings, workshops and try-outs of new dramatic work. During readings and workshops, a play will undergo transformations, sometimes radical, before finally being presented in a major, often commercial, venue. This was definitely the case with both *Millennium Approaches* and *Perestroika*.

Readings, workshops and productions (US and UK)

Tony Kushner began working on *Millennium Approaches* in 1987 as commissioned by the Eureka Theatre Company in San Francisco: a company devoted to political, especially epic, theatre. Oskar Eustis, then artistic director of the Eureka, met Kushner after a perform-ance of *A Bright Room Called Day* in New York in 1985, and he immediately recognized Kushner's talent. Eustis directed the first professional production of *A Bright Room Called Day* in San Francisco in the fall of 1987 and following this production, the theatre com-missioned Kushner to write a new play, eventually to become *Mil-lennium Approaches* (Weber, 1993). Kushner describes Oskar Eustis's influence on the play as tremendous; in fact Kushner wrote it directly for him to direct (Jones, 1998: 158).

Initially, as commissioned by the Eureka, *Angels in America* was intended to be something quite different from what it eventually turned out to become. Oskar Eustis has recorded it as being intended as a short and humorous play with serious underlying issues. He has described his reaction when he saw the first draft: 'We were terribly excited about this 90-minute comedy. But then in the fall of 1988, the first draft came in and we knew that we were in trouble' (Weber, 1993). Obviously Eustis and the company had had other expecta-tions for the piece, while Kushner had become intent on fulfilling his own vision of a much longer, deeper and more complicated play.

The first reading of the manuscript took place at the New York Theatre Workshop in November of 1988. Following that, since Eustis had accepted a job at the Mark Taper Forum in Los Angeles, the play was developed there. During the process at the Mark Taper

Forum it became obvious that the play should be split in two parts, so in the spring of 1990 a workshop production was presented of *Millennium Approaches,* directed by Eustis and designed by Mark Wedlend. Further changes and revisions took place and then, in May 1991, *Millennium Approaches* received its world premiere at the Eureka directed by David Esbjornson and designed by Tom Kann.

While *Millennium Approaches* had been workshopped and in rehearsal, Kushner had been writing on *Perestroika,* which was performed at the Eureka only as a staged reading following the full performance of *Millennium Approaches* (Román, 1998: 204–205). Director David Esbjornson recalls that the production situation was an odd one, because of unresolved conflicts between Kushner, Eustis and the Eureka. Nevertheless, talking to the *New York Times* in 1993 he describes the job as one of his best productions, despite a low production budget resulting in small catastrophes like collapsing scenery (Weber, 1993). However, *Perestroika* was far from done (at the time it ended with all the characters standing at the foot of the Empire State Building when an atomic bomb explodes), and it was obvious after the reading at Eureka that the play needed extensive work. Though the Eureka production was fairly well received by local critics, Broadway producers remained wary of the play, partly because of fear of controversy over its subject matter, and partly because of its large technical demands (Fisher, 2002: 60). Following the production *Perestroika* was taken back to the drawing board for further workshopping under Eustis's direction at the Mark Taper Forum, while *Millennium Approaches* went to London to be performed at the National Theatre which turned out to be a major critical success.

Millennium Approaches opened at the National Theatre in London on 23 January 1992. The performance played at the Cottesloe, essentially a black box and the smallest space at the National Theatre, seating 300. Declan Donnellan, who is primarily known for his work on Shakespeare and seventeenth-century theatre, was chosen to direct the play. The choice of Donnellan to direct the show seemed strange on the surface as he had never worked with a contemporary living playwright before. However, Kushner's sprawling play is not unsuited to the Shakespearean theatre. John M. Clum sees connections to Shakespeare's romantic comedies in *Angels in America*, and Art Borreca has pointed to the particular combination of Shakespeare and Brecht in the British theatre from the mid-1900s claiming that 'Donnellan's production of *Angels* demonstrated that the English synthesis of the "Shakespearean" and the "Brechtian" is still a vital one' (Borreca, 1997: 245; Clum, 2000: 249). While the American productions had struggled with the play's Brechtian qualities and elements, Donnellan's production seemed to have no trouble visualizing the dialectic and contrapuntal structure of the play. Donnellan collaborated with Nick Ormerod on the set design, and they decided on a solution that would highlight the American nature of the play in a playful way while also commenting on itself.

For the production of *Millennium Approaches,* Donnellan and Olmerod decided to keep the stage bare and black except for a Jasper Johns-like painting of an American flag on the back wall. All scenes and actions took place in front of this flag. Kushner recalls having second thoughts about the set. In the *New York Times* he said 'I thought "Oh, God, they don't really like the play – they just want to do this play to knock America"' (Weber, 1993). Rather than 'knocking' America though, the production sought to frame, or give an abstracted idea of, America; illustrating Belize's charge against Louis that what he really cares about is not the real America, but the idea of America (Borreca, 1998: 253). In this way, Borreca observes, the London production truly fulfilled Brecht's notion that a performance should visualize the obscured reality behind the action. By framing the stage itself in a representation of an idea of America, *Millennium Approaches* took on new meanings. On this empty playing field, the characters and stage hands wheeled in and out only the most necessary elements. The changes of scenery thereby became part of the process of the play, truly constructing the actor-driven event wished for by Kushner, who also ultimately came to love the performance. Seeing the show after the second preview, Kushner said, 'It had blossomed in a way that hadn't seemed possible' (Weber, 1993).

With the strong critical acclaim from London making its way back to America, the buzz surrounding the play grew noticeably bigger and an increasing number of producers began showing interest in it. However, with critical acclaim, came pressure: The pressure on Eustis and Kushner to produce something extraordinary in the first complete production of the play at the Mark Taper Forum.

The team had the difficult task of producing both plays, of which *Perestroika* was still in a constant phase of revision, in a short period of time. Work had already been done on *Millennium Approaches* at both the Taper and at the Eureka, and rehearsals for the play were going well. However, as was to be the case with most theatres taking on both plays, *Perestroika* seemed to be problematic both for the directors and the actors, who had to be in rehearsal for the play while also performing in something else at night. During the rehearsal process, Kushner was still writing the play which of course added to the actors' challenges. Kushner recalls the problems with *Perestroika* which ultimately received mixed reviews in the Los Angeles production. He outlines how he and others had problems with the structure of the play, initially written in five acts. Some people around him felt that the play needed to have stronger similarities with *Millennium Approaches*, so Kushner transformed the play to a three-act structure, thereby undoing part of *Perestroika*'s more fluid or journey-like nature (Jones, 1998: 160). Ultimately Kushner realized this as a mistake, and once *Perestroika* reached Broadway, it returned to a five-act structure.

The Los Angeles production was very well received in general with most critics focusing their praise on *Millennium Approaches*. Having been bedazzled by the British production, Frank Rich, however, was more sceptical of this production describing the staging as 'at times stodgy', and 'plodding', and called *Perestroika* 'a somewhat embryonic, occasionally overstuffed, mixture of striking passages, Talmudic digressions and glorious epiphanies' (Rich, 1992).

Between these productions and the British production of *Millennium Approaches* in January of 1992, the two parts had literally been seen by thousands of people over 2 years (Román, 1998: 205). This means that, though the Taper production was in essence the first full performance of both plays, the play had received ample attention during its long process and was awaited with great expectations. 1992 was also election year in America and in the elections, held in early November, Bill Clinton, a Democrat, was elected to replace George H. W. Bush as president of the USA after 12 years of Republican presidencies. As we saw in the last chapter, Frank Rich alluded to this political change in his review of the New York performance of *Millennium Approaches*. In the years it took to write and produce these different versions of *Angels in America,* America itself had changed.

Following the Taper production it was clear that *Angels in America* was heading to Broadway in spite of a tentative earlier agreement to perform the play at the Public Theater in New York City, which has a history of performing socially conscious and political material. The major theatre producing organizations in New York competed over the rights to the play and it was announced that instead of moving the Taper production, the play would have a new director and designer. In other words, though several of the central actors remained the same, a completely new production of *Angels in America* was to be staged within just 2 years of the official opening in San Francisco. New York director and playwright George C. Wolf was chosen to direct the production which had design by Robin Wagner. This production ultimately landed excellent reviews for both plays and earned numerous Tony nominations and awards for the cast, creative team and Kushner. It was also, compared to other so-called 'straight plays' (meaning 'not musicals') at the time, one of the most expensive productions in Broadway History. The production cost $3.7 million to mount with a running cost of about $200,000 a week. It was estimated that it would have to run a year or more on Broadway to recoup the investments made (Weber, 1994a). In the end, the production turned out to be tremendously successful and reached a large audience; *Millennium Approaches* ran for 20 previews and 367 performances and *Perestroika* for 217 performances and 26 previews (IBDB.com). Its producers did not make much money on the Broadway production, but as a result of the national tour, national and international productions and the TV version, they have ultimately done so.

International productions

Angels in America is a fundamentally American play in terms of its subject matter and its many references to culture, history and politics. Despite this it has received a wealth of international attention and keeps being produced around the world. Most theatres will create a program with notes that explain the many references and supply a historical background of America in 1980s to offset an international audience's lack of familiarity with the specifics of the play. Though the play in general has been well received, a certain scepticism towards America and its politics dominates much of the international critical discourse.

Danish productions

In February and March of 1995 both *Millennium Approaches* and *Perestroika* were performed in two different Danish cities. Aarhus Teater, the leading regional theatre, premiered *Millennium Approaches* on 10 February, while the Royal Theatre in Copenhagen (the national theatre) premiered *Millennium Approaches* on 17 February with *Perestroika* following only 2 weeks later. The arrival of *Angels in America* on the Danish stage was without doubt the cultural event of the theatrical season. All leading newspapers published features on the plays and reviews of European productions that preceded the Danish ones. Expectations, similar to those expressed in America, that the plays held the magical power to somehow transform the theatre were prevalent.

In the newspaper criticism, however, it becomes clear that the performances did not succeed completely. The plays, considered as texts, are described as masterpieces of the American theatre, but the Danish productions did not realize the texts' potential. The history, the different religions and the political system seemed too foreign. The identities represented by the different characters were read as too particularly American and thus too different for a Danish audience to really care about the characters' conflicts – the argument went. This disappearance of immediate identification meant that the performances ran the risk of being unable to maintain an audience's interest in the characters, making them seem less universally human and more like American curiosities, according to some critics. Instead of disrupting or deconstructing the notion of a particular, unified, melting-pot America, the performances seem to have reified an already existing notion of America, however skewed or prejudiced that notion might be. The performance of the American nation performed in *Angels in America* confirmed what the Danish critics already thought they knew about America and the relations between politics, organized religion, AIDS and male homosexuality. This is identical to some German critics' reaction (described below) and points to both the ever prevalent anti-American sentiment in Europe and the way America, or rather an idea of America, is ingrained in Western popular culture. It also illustrates perfectly how difficult it is to take a play as specifically American as *Angels in America* and transplant it to a different cultural and political climate.

The performances in Aarhus of *Millennium Approaches* and of both plays in Copenhagen got a wide variety of reviews. All three productions received both positive and more critical reviews. The Aarhus production was performed as a chamber piece, not unlike the Cottesloe production in England, in a smaller house with a more intimate setting. The Royal Theatre production was performed in a larger traditional theatre making use of the proscenium. These productions then both highlight the theatrical possibilities and problems in the cultural translation of a play as culturally specific as *Angels in America*.

Performing the play in a country that considers itself liberated in relation to the acceptance of alternative sexualities and lifestyles, as is the case in Denmark, obviously changes the dynamics of the performance. That both theatres also to some extent tried to universalize the topic by focusing the play on the domestic tribulations of the two couples can be seen from the criticism. The Aarhus production will serve as an example.

In Aarhus the play was performed on a small bare stage. The stage consisted of a bare stone-like platform getting slightly narrower towards the back, a wing on either side and steps in front (Holm, 1995: 32). One critic called it a 'concrete desert' (Lund, 1995). The director, Johan Bergenstråhle, chose to focus on the interpersonal relationships between the characters and thereby downplayed the larger political and historical issues. Danish theatre scholar Bent Holm notes how the performance used the body as a recurring metaphor for the characters and their relationships leading to a transformation in which 'the verbal dimension – the intellectual, sophisticated wit – was toned down, as was the detailed description of the external world. Thus the priority was moved from exterior and intellectual drama to interior and physical drama' (Holm, 1995: 35). In doing this the director seems to have de-emphasized the gay aspect of the play to the extent that Joe and Harper became the one central couple. Critic Me Lund describes this in her review and suggests that, in this production, Prior and Louis seem to be nothing but a contrasting mirror image to Joe and Harper and that this focus makes Joe's struggle with his sexuality and his complex father/ son relationship with Roy Cohn the central conflict of the play. She asks 'why perform precisely this play, if it is the white heterosexual male's fear of his inner gay man that is the theme?' (Lund, 1995). Obviously this transformed the play and while the performance managed to carry on its investigation of America as a cultural and political threshold, for some of the critics, the downplaying of the gay aspects fundamentally changed the play into a study of a heterosexual relationship, however volcanic, instead of a gay fantasia.

German productions

In the year following the American openings of *Angels in America,* the play, particularly *Millennium Approaches,* received numerous German productions (e.g. Zurich, Hamburg, Essen and Frankfurt). As was the case with the Danish productions of the play, word had already reached Germany about this new American theatrical sensation. However, some curiosity as to what the fuss was about can be seen here as well. In a review of the National Theatre production, performed on tour in Germany in November of 1992, critic C. Bernd Sucher expresses his doubts as to what exactly the play has to offer a German audience. He calls the play 'the answer for the theatre of Dallas and Denver. Instead of rich, dumb, scheming heteros we see poor, wise, homos with integrity. A gay fantasia in episodes' (Sucher, 1992). In a review of the New York production, Joerg von Uthmann suggests that at the centre of *Angels in America* we find two homosexual couples: one in which the partners leave each other and one in which the partners cannot find each other. This obviously refers to Louis and Prior, and Joe and Roy Cohn (Uthmann, 1993). Unlike the far more typical reading of the play, in which we have a heterosexual and a gay couple at the centre, or the Danish reading with Harper and Joe at the centre, Uthmann's reading completely relegates the female characters to a secondary position and thereby shifts the balance of the play. However, it does point to the different constellations of homoeroticism at the core of the play, and makes it, truly, a gay play concerned primarily with gay issues. Uthmann is not particularly impressed with the play, however. He asks why the Broadway interest is so great since the American theatre, unlike the German theatre, has seen plenty of plays dealing with questions of AIDS: William Hoffman's *As Is*, Larry Kramer's *The Normal Heart* and *Destiny of Me*, Cheryl Weston's *Before It Hits Home*, Paula Vogel's *The Baltimore Waltz*, William Finn's *Falsettos* and Paul Rudnick's *Jeffrey*. Though most of these plays would be unfamiliar to a German readership in the early 1990s, Uthmann answers his own question by claiming that in each of the other plays we are given an individual story of disease without connecting this to a larger issue. In *Angels in America*, according to Uthmann, AIDS is a collective disease functioning as a metaphor for a diseased society. Despite this recurring pathologization of America by linking the US as a nation to AIDS, Uthmann offers an interesting thematic reading of the relation between the formation of a nation and an international disease. However, his interesting reading did not necessarily translate into performances in Germany.

In a comparative review of four productions, the theatre critic for the respected theatre magazine, *Theater Heute*, Franz Wille, analyses the differences between four productions. Wille points out a central if somewhat surprising premise: that *Angels in America* does not tell a German audience anything it didn't already know about America or AIDS. As we saw in the Danish criticism, this is a recurring observation. Where the Danish critics generally agreed that the translation, done by poet Morti Wizki, was excellent, Wille points out that the different German translations were problematic. Wille makes clear that the play took even longer in German due to the language and this, in the performances that stayed loyal to the text, created performances that were simply too long. The performances in Zurich, Hamburg and Essen all stayed close to the text where the performance in Frankfurt radically changed the text.

The Zurich performance, directed by Volker Hesse, took place in a small theatre, the Zuericher Neumarkt-Theater. The small auditorium was divided by a platform stage on which the action took place. As in most other performances the focus was on the actors, who, however, seem to have performed in a superficial, external and clichéd fashion. Using the character of Roy Cohn as an example, Wille points out how Christian Schneller used American TV as an example of how to play his character. He says 'Schneller plays Roy Cohn as you might imagine a nasty, ambitious, American lawyer, if you mainly know about nasty American lawyers from lousy American TV series [. . .]' (Wille, 1995: 56). The local critic did not have kinder words for the show. C. Bernd Sucher, critic for *Sueddeutsche Zeitung*, called this performance of *Angels in America* a 'theatre version of the gay hit: I am what I am', compares it to *Charley's Aunt*, and calls it a piece of kitchy, bad, writing (Sucher, 1993). Hubert Spiegel says that 'Kushner's play is a pointy homo-operetta, a trivial tragedy about marriage, a Republican pandemonium, an angry fairy tale of Reagan's children, and a portrait of the homosexual gay-basher Roy Cohn' (Spiegel, 1993).

The Hamburg production, directed by Werner Schroeter and performed in a much larger space at the Deutsches Schauspielhaus, was performed on a traditional stage with interlocking platforms in front of a stylized skyscraper with a wading pool in front. Grander in scale than the Zurich production, the set seemed to diminish the actors in scale forcing them to primarily act on the front stage in what Wille describes as 'large, if false, emotions' (Wille, 1995: 57). The main problem with the production, however, seems to have been its fear of its gayness: its unwilling homophobia. Wille identifies a lack of homoeroticism between the characters that renders the whole performance unbelievable and hard to understand. As with the Danish production from Aarhus, the refocusing of the play away from its depiction of gay love, sex and death, creates an unbalance that, eventually, radically alters the show. The highly stylized and effeminate performance of Belize, according to Wille 'transplants *Angels in America* to where it least of all belongs: in the middle-class fantasy land of a transsexual honky-tonk' (Wille, 1995: 57–58).

All is, however, not lost in Germany. The modern German theatre, in a tradition from Piscator, Brecht and the theatrical modernist avant-garde, has a tradition of producing radical stagings of plays. The Frankfurt production, directed by Thomas Schulte-Michels, was a radical deviation from the previous German stagings of the play – a sort of The Wooster Group meets *Angels in America* approach to the play. Here the audience saw no representation of New York, met no recognizable psychologically identified characters, and no performances built on, or inspired by, American TV or movies. The characters all used microphones or microports, at times speaking directly to the audience, spoke in a ferocious tempo, and would, since the text had been radically cut, relate the missing scenes to the audience. Wille, and here he reveals his own taste, clearly liked this performance the best. In Brecht's homeland, however, it does seem appropriate that the acting should be illustrative instead of naturalized.

Japanese productions

Over the past 15 years American movie and stage director Robert Allan Ackerman (not to be confused with Robert Altman who was to direct the movie version of the play) has directed several productions of *Angels in America* in Japan. In 1994 *Millennium Approaches* opened in Tokyo at the Ginza Saison Theater to be followed by *Perestroika* the following season. In 1979 Ackerman directed the Broadway production of Martin Sherman's *Bent*: a history play about the Nazi persecution of gay men set partly in a concentration camp, in which two incarcerated men fall in love. *Bent*, like *Angels in America*, utilizes the structure of the history play to investigate current themes: in *Bent*'s case, the ongoing discrimination against homosexual people. It also, like *Angels in America*, uses Brechtian devices, so Ackerman was no stranger to gay plays, the history play as a genre, Brechtian devices, or political messages. Ackerman, at the time of the 1994 production, clearly saw *Angels in America* delivering a political message of tolerance which he expected the play to bring to Japan. He said:

> I hope the play will make the Japanese more aware of AIDS and homosexuality. When the international AIDS conference was held in Yokohama, I watched the news on TV in the United States. There were a lot of reports about the strong resistance to dealing with the issue in Japan. (Mizui, 1994)

Downplaying the fact that the issues relating to AIDS and homosexuality in the play are particularly American, Ackerman's first production in Tokyo interpreted the play in a universal fashion with Ackerman saying that 'The main message of *Angels in America* is one of passion and universality of love' (Mizui, 1994). Ackerman took issues with the George C. Wolf's Broadway production, which he found to be too realistic, and he wanted the Japan production to focus more on the fantastic elements of the play and pay special attention to the play's genre as a gay fantasia. Seeing the play as displaying a certain sense of optimism and belief in progress that Ackerman connected to the change in the American administration and the early years of the Clinton presidency, Ackerman's production strived to achieve a certain lightness and magical quality. The set design, for example, consisted of a number of light tubes, crystal angels, shiny steel rods and stars twinkling (Tanaka, 2004b). The lightness of the set corresponded to the play's depiction of progress.

Ten years later, in 2004, Ackerman directed the play again, this time for a newly founded company called Theatre Project Tokyo (TPT). In 2003 Ackerman had directed the company's initiation, a well-received performance of *Bent*, and he kept working with the same actors for *Angels in America* the following year. This time around, however, Ackerman's view of the play was slightly different. In an interview he said about the first production:

> There was more of a certain naivete [*sic*] about it 10 years ago. As I said, I think then we thought AIDS would be gone in 10 years, and I think now that the magnitude of it and the destruction is even greater than it was then, and politically I understand a lot more about the play than I did then. (Tanaka, 2004a)

Expanding on the political change in his production, Ackerman says that 'this production is in some ways more cynical than the first one' (Tanaka, 2004a). Part of this cynicism is due to world politics (and particularly the American domination of them) and it made Ackerman focus this performance differently paying closer attention to the individual and the individual's potential for change. This clearly refocuses the performance, as each character became individualized in contrast to a more collective fathoming of change. The design also reflected this somewhat more cynical or bleak outlook.

The TPT's space is a converted dye boiler room converted into a black box. In this industrial setting, designer Bobby Wojewodski created a stark empty space consisting of a grey stage in front of the exposed back wall with electric wires strung along it. A tower of scaffolding was set at one side of the stage. Long white drapes with images of angels were strung along the seats in the auditorium to create a contrast between the stark and dark stage image and the lighter audience space, possibly relating to Ackerman's belief that change would start with the individual audience member. In the middle of the back wall an existing fire door was used to reveal another space where the different sub-plots were performed. With the door open, two worlds could exist at the same time. The loud noise of the door slamming was used to refocus the audience's attention back to the main stage. Music by gay icons in American culture such as Maria Callas, Judy Garland and Billie Holiday was used in a similar fashion, but also to underscore the American nature of the play. The scaffolding, often used in Brecht's perform-ances as a way of pointing to the materiality of the stage, was used for what a reviewer called 'slightly grotesque, transvestite-type angels who sit atop the tower and deliver insights into the lives below' (Tanaka, 2004b). Most of the young actors, chosen from workshops Ackerman gave (and still gives with what has now become known as 'the company'), all received excellent notices, particularly for the way they managed to perform as a company and still point to the individualization of the characters. Akira Yamamoto as Roy Cohn and Naoki Saito as Prior gave particularly strong performances.

In 2007 TPT revived the show and Ackerman recalled the suc-cess of the last show in an interview with *The Daily Yomiuri*. He said that 'You couldn't get a ticket last time. It was impossible' (Matsuoka, 2007). The first two productions of the play, he says, were 'focused on the onset of AIDS in the 1980s and the attendant theme of death'. However, by working on the revival he has come to realize that the play is really 'a play about life and living' (Matsuoka, 2007).

Angels in America – the movie
In 2003 the American cable TV network HBO aired its star-studded $60 million adaptation of *Angels in America* directed by Mike Nichols, director of *Who's Afraid of Virginia Woolf, The Graduate, The Birdcage, Closer* and recently *Charlie Wilson's War*, with a screen-play by Kushner. In two parts, the TV production mirrored the theatrical production and had a running time of about six and a half hour total. It was the TV event of the year and swept the Emmys, dominated the Golden Globes, and won a slew of other awards for its direction, acting and writing. Ten years after its Broadway pre-miere, *Angels in America* was once more centre place in the American imagination. The broadcast garnered, as had been the case with the stage version a decade earlier, almost unanimous praise, and this time the show had the potential of reaching a far larger audience.

HBO broadcast the show to about 30 million homes in the US, which is a potentially larger audience than most dramatic work will ever reach (Abramovich, 2003). The HBO production had been a decade in the making.

With its epic scope, intense visual elements and other cinematic qualities, *Angels in America* initially seemed destined to become a movie. Quickly following the American performances of the play, talks began between Kushner and American director of film, theatre and TV Robert Altman: director of movies like *The Long Good Bye*, *Nashville*, *Come Back to the Five and Dime Jimmy Dean Jimmy Dean*, *Short Cuts* and *A Prairie Home Companion*. In writing *Angels in America*, Kushner had been particularly inspired by Altman's movie *Nashville* (1975) with its epic structure of independent yet connected stories weaving together, and he specifically sought to get Altman to direct the project feeling that he, if any, could do the play justice for the screen. Kushner trusted Altman to make the cinematic version different from the play: to make it an independent piece of art and not 'just' a filmed version of the play (Davidson, 1998: 139).

From the beginning of their collaboration Kushner and Altman were aware that turning *Angels in America* into a typical, or marketable, studio release would be difficult because of the length of the play, which in performance runs somewhere between 7 and 8 hours. They discussed doing two 3-hour releases, but when they had trouble finding a studio to agree to the project, they discussed doing it for cable, which, eventually, 10 years later turned out to become the solution. Altman, however, eventually left the project and moved on to making other movies. He pointed out how Kushner used cinematic techniques in his playwriting, and how this presented a problem for translating the play to the screen, as what had seemed novel in the theatre – the cross-cutting, people talking at the same time, simultaneity in scenes, visual elements such as flaming letters, steel books and falling angels – had all been done on film before.

Translating not just the play, but also its novel form, presented a challenge to Altman as it did, eventually, to Mike Nichols as well. Kushner worked closely with Altman for a year and a half developing a screenplay, but studio executives were reluctant to accept the material because of its subject matter, the budget and the length, and eventually plans for a cinematic release were dropped (Greenman, 2003). Then in 2001 it was reported that HBO had picked up the play with Mike Nichols as director and was in negotiations with a possible cast. Nichols originally planned six 1-hour episodes which loosely correspond to six acts. When finally shown, however, the show aired in two parts with each lasting about 3 hours.

Despite a few bad reviews, (the *Washington Times* called it 'bombastic and hollow' (Grenier, 2003)), most critics showered the show with same accolades that it had received a decade earlier, many remarking that the very fact that *Angels in America* could now be shown on TV was indeed in itself a comment on the progress of the country.

The TV version in a moment of cinematic grandeur opens with a significant comment on the show itself. In bird's eye perspective the camera hovers above San Francisco before travelling across the continent – over Utah via Chicago to New York – ending up in Central Park as the Angel of the Bethesda Fountain, where the characters are to gather in the epilogue. As the Angel lands and settles into her frozen position as a statue, she turns her head towards the audience, showing signs of life, indicating that even things that seem solid may change. In one opening shot we are made aware of the tremendous ambition of the play – its demand that we consider this about America and not only about the characters portrayed naturalistically in the movie. This naturalistic acting presented the biggest problem to the few who were critical of the TV version. Unlike the stage version, the characters were presented completely naturalistically without the Brechtian elements of acting and the theatre to put the performance in perspective. Cinema, and even more so TV, is a very different medium than the theatre. The magic that appeared as magic on stage does not maintain its quality on screen, however beautifully done. We are used to seeing angels fly in movies, but not on stage. In the theatre we are always aware that it is a real person flying, while we know from experience that in movies anything can happen. This is a crucial difference making *Angels in America*, the TV version, a somewhat smaller play than the stage version.

If the loss of magic made the TV version a smaller play it also, arguably, made it a less political one. Gretchen E. Minton and Ray Schultz point this out in a careful analysis of the reductions made in the text for the HBO version. They find that the reductions in the text, necessary to make the sprawling stage play a movie, are primarily done to take out the larger political, historical, sociological and specifically queer implications of the play. *Angels in America*, the TV version, in their analysis ends up as a more conventional, psychological and straight play than the queerer stage version. It is, as they say, 'Steven Spielberg, [*sic*] and not Bertolt Brecht who exerts the strongest stylistic influence over *Angels*' television adaptation' (Minton and Schultz, 2006: 41).

Though the TV version might have empathized the personal, emotional and fantastic elements and thereby diminished the political and queer aspects of the play, *Angels in America* proved to still have a message for America. The play once again captivated the nation's imagination and despite its flaws the HBO production turned out to be enormously effective. In the decade between the play and the HBO version, America changed in profound ways under a democratic president: AIDS treatment became more efficient, the Cold War faded into memory and though often demonized during election campaigns in America gay men and lesbians slowly gained visibility in the legal system. Tony Kushner celebrates change in

Angels in America and it is only fitting that the play would change over time; shedding layers of meaning while gaining new insights for a new audience in a different time. As a history play, *Angels in America* will undoubtedly keep shedding old and accumulating new layers of historical complexity.

4 Workshopping the Play

This chapter offers a series of practical workshop ideas and exercises based on *Angels in America*. It involves discussion of the play's characters, conflicts, key scenes, motifs and ideas which a group of actors or students could explore practically. The content is informed by previously published interviews with the playwright, actors and directors involved in productions of the play.

Angels in America is an answer, not to a specific question or a specific challenge, but to another play and its context. This is a technique that Kushner learned from Brecht, who would often write a new text as a response to a text he had either seen or read and with which he disagreed. *Angels in America* is a direct response to William Hoffman's AIDS-play *As Is* which Kushner saw and, in his words, 'hated' (Savran, 1996: 301). Kushner describes the process:

> When I started *Angels*, I started it, following Brecht who always did this, as an answer: you find a play that makes you mad – either you love that it makes you mad or you think it's abominable – and needs to be responded to. (Savran, 1996: 301)

It is also, however, an answer to the challenge of AIDS, life in the 1980s in America, and the seemingly futile efforts of identity politics at the time. While working with *Angels in America* as an actor, a director, a dramaturge or a set-designer it is important to always keep the play's dialogical origin in mind. The play is written not just *in* dialogue but also *as* a dialogue. This dialectic informs the play's structure (short scenes centred in a conflict), but also the way the dialogue is constructed as an argument.

Angels in America is an ambitious, sprawling, anarchistic play that points in many directions and contains an endless number of references to culture, history, philosophy and politics. To account for them all in production is probably impossible, but it is, of course, important that the actors know the references in order to understand the universe in which the play takes place. Besides giving ideas for exercises that student actors/directors can use in working with the play, much of the text below will be aimed at giving practical exercises clarifying *Angels in America* in relation to the many references used in the play. The exercises develop from exploring the context of the play, to manifesting this in a set design in which the actors can explore the characters. After establishing this, the exercises will help develop the characters through focusing on language and then movement before using these elements to explore the central conflicts and motifs.

First impression

When starting out working on a play, either as an actor, director, dramaturge or designer, the first impression is very important. This is perhaps especially true for the actor. The first sense of a character can be a very valuable tool later in the process when it can be hard to remember the initial meeting with the play. Konstantin Stanislavski, the influential Russian theatre director and acting teacher, says that 'You cannot erase a spoiled first impression any more than you can recover lost maidenhood' (Stanislavski, 1961: 7). Keep this in mind as you read through the play the first time. Make notes of your impression afterwards. Then, put the notes away until later in the process when, after working intensely on the play, you might need to be reminded of that first reaction.

The world of the play

The task of producing *Angels in America* is a daunting one. The marathon length, the complicated matter, the stage magic called for in the play, the number of characters played by only eight actors, the long speeches, the jumps in time and the split scenes all present their own obstacles and challenges to any creative team taking on fulfilling Kushner's theatrical vision. There have been as many different rehearsal processes as there have been productions of the play(s) and each one has defined and worked with the play(s) in its own way. Any director working with the play will obviously need to conduct a certain amount of research into the theory and context informing the play and its dramatic universe. However, this is also necessary for the actor. It has been said about Konstantin Stanislavski that:

> When working on a play, Stanislavsky [*sic*], the director was always striving to discover its central social, ideological, and philosophical problem. He demanded from the actor and director a thorough knowledge of the play's material – of its historic, philosophic, and political character. (Gorchakov, 1954: 394)

This 'thorough knowledge' helps the director conceptualize the performance, making it a consistent whole, but would also, Stanislavski insisted, let the actor formulate the character within the concept of the play, its themes and its context. Keeping this advice from one of the founding directors of the twentieth-century theatre in mind, the following is intended as a series of exercises (to be used individually or in groups) for student directors and actors working on the play.

Understanding the dramatic universe

Tony Kushner created a version of America in the 1980s in *Angels in America*. Though this world has many references to, and similarities with, the 'real' America (more specifically New York City of the 1980s) it remains fictional in the way it functions as a dramatic frame for the characters' actions, emotions, crises and ultimate development. In order to work with the text in its complexity it is necessary to capture the distinction between the 'real' and the 'constructed' in both the play's meaning and its characters. For the actor working with the play, however, no matter how historically real a character, an event, or a line is, the situation is always fictitious: a construction of an imagined world in which their character lives and interacts with the peculiar (and particular) logic of the specific play. With a political play like *Angels in America*, and as we've seen Kushner strongly defines this work as political, it is particularly important that the directors/actors relate the imagined world to the real world that the play is attempting to reflect upon and make an intervention within.

When the cast comes together the first time to read the play it is helpful if the director, the dramaturge or the cast-members have gathered questions (and/or materials) about events and people mentioned in the text such as:

1. elements they don't know about and feel it is important to understand;
2. comments that strike them as odd or represent a political point of view with which they either agree or disagree (the stronger the agreement or disagreement the better);
3. fantastic or religious symbols, meanings, actions that they don't understand; or moments of particular density that they feel need to be explained.

It is likely that all the questions raised in a discussion like this will be the same as the audience will ask themselves in the process of watching the play. All of the questions or comments need not be explained on the first day of rehearsal, but creating a collective list early in the rehearsal process will lead to immediate or later discussions about the play's dramatic world. This will throughout the

rehearsal or workshop create understanding of the politically, reli-
giously, ethnically and sexually conditioned universe that *Angels in
America* both projects and takes place within.

Depending on the director's strategy this can be done with the
whole play (though this would be quite time consuming) or with
individual scenes. One example could be act 2, scene 6 in *Millennium Approaches* in which Roy and Joe are having lunch with Martin
Heller (described as a Reagan Administration Justice Department
flackman, which might need its own explanation).

Though this scene initially may seem tangential to the play's
depiction of two couples in turmoil it is essential to the discussion,
definition and critique of Reagan era politics and lack of ethics that
the play raises. Martin Heller's opening speech, for example, is basically a litany of references to: the Supreme Court, affirmative action,
abortion, defence, Central America, family values, a live investment
climate, having the White House locked till 2000, a permanent fix
on the Oval Office, getting the Senate back, the South delivering
the House, the end of Liberalism, the end of New Deal Socialism,
the end of secular humanism, and the emergence of a genuinely
American personality modelled on Reagan (69). As the scene goes
on this discussion lays out Roy's belief in politics as the 'game of
being alive' and portrays, critically, what Kushner sees as the cor-
ruption of power. Many of the references will be hard to understand
for the audience (particularly if the play is produced in an international setting) and though only in direct connection to the characters
of Roy and Joe, the politics are important for the other characters'
development – particularly for Louis who is constructed as the
opposite of Roy, Joe and Martin Heller's philosophy.

After reading each scene (or speech, depending on the division of
the text) ask:

- What is the importance of the reference?
- What does it tell us about the world in which the play takes place?

- How does the reference influence the characters in the scene or what does it tell us about the characters?
- How does it relate to the politics of the play?
- How do we create a theatrical universe in which we can illustrate these theories?

Visualizing the themes of *Angels in America*

Reading *Angels in America* is one thing, seeing it is another. Every drama intended for performance needs to be visualized. In the transformation from text to stage a play changes rapidly and *Angels in America* is a highly visual play with different separate worlds merging, angels flying, books appearing, and so forth. There have been many more or less successful solutions to the design challenges raised by *Angels in America*. Tony Kushner gives a note about the staging saying:

> The play benefits from a pared-down style of presentation, with minimal scenery and scene shifts done rapidly (no blackouts!), employing the cast as well as stagehands – which makes for an actor-driven event as this must be. The moments of magic – the appearance and disappearance of Mr. Lies and the ghosts, the Book hallucination, and the ending – are to be fully realized, as bits of wonderful theatrical illusion – which means it's OK if the wires show, and maybe it's good that they do, but the magic should at the same time be thoroughly amazing. (11)

Having previously talked about this note, in terms of its Brechtian implications in 'letting the wires show' and thereby pointing to itself as theatre, the other important implication in this note is the way the design should allow the actors to drive the performance. As an 'actor-driven event' the design needs to create a space that is versatile enough to not hinder the actors' performance and allow them to create the almost dreamlike flow of scenes.

The set design of any production of *Angels in America* then needs to be flexible enough to accommodate: rapidly shifting scenes without interrupting the flow (no blackout!), a combination of realistic and fantastic scenes and a sense of the external setting. Arnold Aronson formulates this in his article 'Design for *Angels in America*: Envisioning the Millennium' saying that there are two fundamental questions when creating a visual concept for a play.

1. Where are we and how can this be visualized? This, obviously is a central scenographic question.
2. How can this practically be done within our budget and time?

Angels in America is ambitious in scope and any design of it is forced to be the same. (Kushner nods to the second question in his introduction to *Perestroika* when he says if 'you plan to have an airborne Angel, which is a good thing, be warned: It's incredibly hard to make the flying work. Add a week to tech time' (143)). However, with *Angels in America* the design should also attempt to condense the meaning of the play and illustrate this physically. Pointing out that *Angels in America* is of course set in New York in the 1980s, Aronson asks the all-important question 'How does one present the idea of "America"? Is there an obvious imagistic or emblematic representation? Is there a single icon, perhaps, that will provide the audience with a sense of time, place, tone, and point of view?' (Aronson, 1997: 213).

Aronson supplies three different examples of design choices. The design by Nick Ormerod at the National Theatre in London created a background of 'stars and stripes'. The American flag is of course emblematic of the USA for any foreign audience, but it might not carry the same weight for a domestic audience. At the Mark Taper forum in Los Angeles the design by John Conklin evoked classic American architecture by having the back wall be the façade of a house combining elements of a New England meeting-house and

Jeffersonian classicism – both obviously also examples of the radical American democracy that Louis theorizes in the play. However the wall was cracked – symbolizing an ideal that is broken – and the angel flew in through this crack. This design then, though not referring to New York specifically, referred to the fundamental questions of American democracy in the play. The New York production, designed by Robert Wagner, was a neutral stage framed by the proscenium arch and highly mobile black screens creating divisions and room formations on stage. The neutrality of this design, Aronson points out, can be seen in relation to the production being actually in New York, the literal world of the play. A New York audience, Aronson suggests, would be more familiar with the text's references. It would automatically assume that, when Louis is in the park he is in the Rambles in Central Park, and when Harper is at the Brooklyn Promenade an audience would conjure up the image of the impressive New York skyline seen from Brooklyn. (Aronson, 1997: 214–217). As an international production the 1995 production at the Royal Theatre in Copenhagen, Denmark, took a different approach by visually having the scene framed by an imaginary New York skyline; as if the whole play took place in Central Park framed as it is by the towers of the city. The high-rises framing the stage in Copenhagen were futuristic, expressionistic and looked menacingly down on the action. This design choice then highlighted the apocalyptic and threatening sense of breakdown prevalent in *Millennium Approaches* in particular.

Besides finding different ways of letting the stage design convey certain images about America as a nation, several different designs have also attempted to illustrate Benjamin's theory of history that inspired Kushner. Walter Benjamin writes in 'Theses on the Philosophy of History' about the angel:

> Where we perceive a chain of events, he sees one single catastrophe which keeps piling wreckage upon wreckage and hurls it in front of his feet. (Benjamin, 1968: 257)

Noting that *Millennium Approaches* and *Perestroika* are different plays and that their design should reflect this, Kushner says, '*Perestroika* proceeds forward from the wreckage made by the Angel's traumatic entry at the end of *Millennium*. A membrane has been broken; there is disarray and debris' (142). This broken membrane relates to the theory of history blasting open, and the debris relates to the trash gathered around the Angel's feet. Illustrations of this have been attempted in several different ways in productions.

The Broadway production of *Perestroika* operated with a scrim through which the audience could watch debris piling up throughout different scenes of the play. In the 2006/2007 British revival at the Lyric Hammersmith Theatre in London, the stage slowly became more and more cluttered through the last acts of *Perestroika*. As the divisions between the 'real' and the 'imaginary' broke down and characters interacted with each other in both realities, the stage grew full of furniture and props. Where the stage would traditionally have been cleared before each new scene, the designer and director had decided to let it fill up, literally, with the debris of the production's own history, obviously as an illustration of Benjamin's thesis. These are but two examples of how a theory can be scenically illustrated.

There are obviously as many ways of visualizing the text as there are productions. Above are only four ways the set has been designed and two ways of illustrating a theory. The following are some ways a group or an individual could work on design related issues. After reading the text all the way through put the text away.

- Putting aside that the play might want to illustrate America to some degree, what are some other words that come to mind. Write down ten words that you associate with the visual world in which the play takes place. These could be framed in terms of colour, emotion or sound – remembering that much modern stage design is done with these elements.

- What are your impressions of the world in which the play takes place? What does this world look like? Is there a particular painting, drawing or movie you can think of that would visualize elements of this?
- Sketch out this initial idea on a piece of paper. After doing that, in groups or alone, go through elements of the text and try to see if your design fulfils both demands to a set as described by Aronson.
- Discuss how characters and/or design elements can be used to illustrate a theory as foundational to the play as the notion of the Angel flying blindly into the future with the trash of history around his feet. Create a concept that would allow you to highlight this in a 'simple pared down way'.
- Find pictures from some of the many productions of *Angels in America* around the world (some of them are presented in the performance history chapter in this book). A simple search on Google will supply plenty of images from productions on all scales. Which of these are closest to your own ideas? Which ones do you like? Which seem to not work so well?
- In a group ponder the following questions: What is the relation between the characters and their world? Which scenes seem most iconographic for the play? What is the function of the image of San Francisco after the earthquake? Should this be used in a design? And, finally, what is the relation between a set and the audience?

Besides designing a set that can illustrate the work and its context the actors also need to relate to the set in a physical, sensual, way. Even before a physical set is constructed an actor can imagine being, as a character, in a set.

- Let all actors lie down on the floor with closed eyes. Let them imagine that they are the Angel falling through the atmosphere.

What does the New York below them look like? What are they about to see when they crash through Prior's bedroom ceiling? What does the set look like from above? How does it feel to be in the different settings for the characters? Stand up, walk around and then lay down again. Let the actors imagine that they are Prior knowing that the Angel is on her way. What does the set feel like from the bed looking up at the ceiling?

This exercise can be repeated endlessly with all the characters. What does it feel like for Harper to enter Antarctica? What does Hannah see when she enters the Pitt apartment? What does Belize's office feel like? Does he relate to Roy's sick-bed in a different way than Prior's? What does Roy's library look like to Ethel when she enters (through the wall, perhaps)? This establishes, in the imagination of the actors, a relation between all the characters and the set regardless of their individual parts.

The language of the play

There are several different kinds of language in *Angels in America*: realistic dialogue, political rants, legal discourse, jokes, poetry, visions, Hebrew, the Angel's metaphysical speeches, accents, dialects, quotes, and so forth. These different kinds of language help give the play its epic feeling, its sprawling and intentionally confusing quality, and its delight in a theatre of rhetoric and discourse. However, it is also demanding for the actors. The following are some suggestions on how to work with the different levels of speech in the play.

Reading

Identify different sections of the text – these can be scenes that you have worked with before in the design/theatrical world section or they can be new scenes – that utilize text in different ways. Some examples of scenes could be:

1. The fast-paced conversation between Roy and Joe in *Millennium Approaches* (act 1, scene 2). Here Roy constantly interrupts himself, talks on the phone, carries several conversations, all the time trying to talk to Joe in between. He curses, jokes, yells, eats and talks politics.

2. The realistic conversation between Emily and Louis in Prior's hospital room in *Millennium Approaches* (act 2, scene 3), during which Louis reveals Prior's ancestry. Typical for the rhythm of Kushner's dialogue, Emily responds to Louis with a humorous remark. The relationship between the serious subject, Louis's anguish, and Emily's annoyance at her mother's habit of embroidery calls for a particular rhythm.

3. Louis's political speech about democracy in America in *Millennium Approaches* (act 3, scene 2) is a particular use of language as well. Besides being a window into the character, which is a very useful and important function of the scene, it also functions on the rhetorical level.

4. The scene between all three Priors in *Millennium Approaches* (act 3, scene 1). This scene is a combination of the different levels of language in the play, for example: regular conversations, riddles, jokes, Hebrew and lyricism.

5. The scene between the Angel, Prior and Belize in *Perestroika* (act 2, scene 2). Being a split scene this scene is particularly useful for studying the relation between different levels of language. There is the conversation between Prior and the Angel, who has her very own and distinct speech pattern, and the conversation between Prior and Belize as Prior relates what happened. This language contains elements of both worlds and thus marks a certain threshold of language.

After identifying the parts of the text that will be used for these reading exercises, have different members of the cast read the parts – it is preferable at this point not to let actors read the parts they will ultimately end up playing. By not having the actors read their own parts you meet two different goals: (1) the actor whose lines are being read by another cast member has a chance to listen to her/his character's words instead of saying them; and (2) all cast members have a chance to engage in the other characters of the play, which force them to consider the play as a whole and not just concentrate on their own parts. This also underscores the play's central dialectic between the collective and the individual. These reading exercises allow the actors to play (and this should be playful) with different voices in characters that they will not be playing (this is quite important for the actors doubling in other characters, who will need to find several voices), but more importantly, the exercises also create ways into the play through which actors can gain an understanding of the underlying rhythms, tensions, themes and politics of the play.

- As you go through the different sections pay special attention to the rhythm of the language. How are the lines supposed to follow each other? Are they fast paced? Are they slow? First, read through the text in a neutral voice and neutral intonation. Pretend that you are reading the news on the BBC or NPR or some other 'serious' news source. Minimize the 'acting'.

  Follow this by having the same actor read the text as she/he thinks it is supposed to be read.

  Follow this by reading the lines in highly inappropriate ways – drunk, in accents/dialects unfit for the character, tired, too fast, in a melodramatic fashion, angry, sexual. The more inappropriate for the particular section the better the exercise will work.

  Each reading – done by a different actor – will reveal something new about the text and free the actor's imagination to

work with the dialogue in a new way, in the end leading to finding the individual character's voice.
- In another reading exercise actors only read the nouns (or verbs, pronouns, etc.) of a monologue or piece of dialogue.

All these exercises can be done sitting around a table or in a circle. They are initial explorations of the language and not, yet, intended for a physical interaction with the play.

Speaking and rhythm

Throughout the play serious political statements are often framed by humour in a way that is indicative of the general rhythm in play. This, obviously, takes a particular timing in order to work on stage. Consider, for example, situations like the following:

> Belize: *You* hate me because you hate black people.
> Louis: I do not. But I do think most black people are anti-Semitic (101).

Or

> Harper: It's terrible. Mormons are not supposed to be addicted to anything. I'm a Mormon.
> Prior: I'm a homosexual.
> Harper: In my church we don't believe in homosexuals.
> Prior: In my church we don't believe in Mormons (38).

While reading through these lines (or some of the many other places in the text) use the exercises from the 'reading section'. Getting the timing of these comedic lines right is essential to the play's unique combination of seriousness and humour (or camp). You may also want to watch camp classics like *Sunset Boulevard*, *Auntie Mame* and *All about Eve*, or the movie version of Harvey Fierstein's *Torch*

Song Trilogy to get a feeling for the particular timing of delivering a one-liner within a conversation.

Speaking in tongues

In several scenes the characters will speak in Hebrew or in another language that may seem unfamiliar to the actors. In *Millennium Approaches*, for example, act 3, scene 2, Emily suddenly speaks in Hebrew instead of English. In *Perestroika*, act 4, scene 9, Ethel Rosenberg sings in Hebrew. These are but a few scenes that include a mixture of English and some other tongue. A few simple exercises will allow actors to work with this. Without suggesting that Hebrew is gibberish, we can make use of non-specific sounds to employ made-up languages.

- In one exercise three actors line up. The actor in the middle must translate for the two other actors who are having a conversation in a language they make up. This should be fast and furious.
- Two actors are having a conversation. Another actor is elected to control the situation and this person decides when the two actors change from English to their made-up language. The actors should continue as fluently as possible between the two languages, maintaining their initial energy.
- One of the actors is giving a political speech at the UN (in a situation not unlike the one that opens *Perestroika*) in a made-up language. Another actor is the translator who must immediately translate the speech into English.

Writing

In order to understand the way the different characters' language identify them it is a good idea to write journal entries for each of them. In a series of short exercises actors pretend to be different characters and write a short journal entry for that character. Use that character's own voice focusing on the language rather than the content.

- What would Louis's entry look like after he leaves Prior in the hospital and attempts to have sex in Central Park?
- What does Harper's entry look like after she comes out of her hallucination with Prior in which she is told that Joe is homosexual?
- What would Roy's journal entry look like (if he had one!) after he learns that he has AIDS?
- What would the Angel's journal entry look like after she learns that Prior doesn't want to be a prophet?

Besides allowing the individual actor to investigate the different characters this exercise pays attention to the different language levels of the play. Throughout the rehearsal process some actors might find it helpful to keep a journal for the character(s) they are playing. This will eventually serve as a log of questions like – what are the different emotions, motives, ideas that the individual character harbours?

The characters of the play

Movement and speech

Building on the exercises on language and the external world of the play it is time to explore the characters in greater depth. Having worked on the language of the different characters already this next set of exercises focuses on the physical side of the character.

- Starting from a particular moment of conflict in a scene, for example: Prior's struggle with the Angel, the Mormon Diorama and Louis's entry, the gathering around the Bethesda fountain in the epilogue, Louis's fight with Joe, Louis and Ethel saying

Kaddish over Roy Cohn with Belize watching, one actor assumes one of the roles and strikes a pose that fits with one of the characters at any moment in the scene. The other cast members, one by one, enter the scene and strike another pose. As actors enter (and it is possible to choose the same character, if so, that actor must touch the 'original' character) a sculpture will be created; a visual interpretation of a moment in that scene. This should be done with a certain speed and is intended to highlight the physicality of each moment in a scene.

- All actors are assigned a character – they should do their own character last. Without speaking they should think of an animal that this character would be. Is Belize a cat, a lioness? Is Roy Cohn a bull dog, a snake? Is Louis a badly behaving puppy? Taking the floor, one by one, the actors should move as their assigned character's animal. Let the 'animals' walk around and react to each other for a little while, then let them use sound but no spoken words. Change character a couple of times (remember the minor characters as well). Then, finally, let the actor do her/his own character.

- An important part of establishing a character is, of course, to figure out how the character moves. Building on the former exercise let the actor work with her/his own character, but instead of creating an animal as interpretation take the character through a series of walks around the room. Imagine the character's walking pattern from childhood to old age. What happens to the movements throughout life? Once the actors have gone through a life span alter the exercise by having them be teenager/sulky, mid-life/tired, old/happy, child/angry, and so on. Once they have gone through this a couple of times identify specific moments in the play. Only the actors whose characters fit in that moment move: Roy and Joe in bar, Hannah and the Angel meet, Harper and Mr Lies discover the Eskimo, Belize and Prior at the court house. Without saying anything or even

necessarily reacting to each other the actors establish the characters' movements as they would be at that specific point in time.
Then ask them to change energy in that particular moment.

This last exercise carries specific challenges for the actors playing
Roy Cohn and Ethel Rosenberg, who, as historical characters, have
documentable ways of moving. Some actors would find it helpful to
look at pictures or, for Roy Cohn TV clips, and try to re-create
those movements or poses. However, it is important to remember
that this is a fictional rendition of the characters. Ron Leibman,
who played Roy Cohn in the New York production, talks about
creating Cohn, the character, in an interview in the *New York Times*.
After describing how, though he didn't want to move like Roy Cohn
in any direct representational way, he did use Roy Cohn's voice and
dialect to capture the character. He says, 'The voice – you can't stay
away from it because it reveals so much about him – is that kind of
whining Bronx nasal thing. [. . .] which is very annoying. But he
was very annoying' (Stevens, 1993). Leibman decided in his physical work with the character that what characterized Cohn was his
voice, marked as it was by geography (whining Bronx nasal thing).
However, another actor might decide that the key to Cohn is the
way he holds himself, or walks, or stands, or sits. These are all physical decisions that the exercises can help the actor make.

As a combination of the reading and physical exercises above
the following exercise allows the actor to try out combinations of
movement and accent.

Several of the characters in the play would (or could) be marked
by using dialects. Hannah, Harper and Joe are all from Salt Lake
City and have lived their lives as faithful Mormons. How does
that set them apart from Louis who, as a Jewish gay man living
in New York City, probably has a different speech pattern? How is
Prior's heritage reflected in his speech? How does Ethel Rosenberg's
older Jewish accent mark her as being from another time? Does it?

How does Belize's accent work alongside Louis's in the diner scene? Is it marked by race or sexuality or both?

- Pick specific moments in the text and let the actors do the physical exercises. Then take the exercises presented in the 'reading section' and work with them in terms of dialect instead. Change the accents. Let Louis speak with Belize's accent and so forth while keeping his own physicality. This will reveal the relation between the actor, the meaning of the text, the physicality of the character and the accent with which that character speaks.

Improvisations

Having worked on how different characters might move and speak, it is time to move onto working on the characters. A central part of Stanislavki's method of acting is to ask questions of the character. Building on this idea, in a series of improvisations, imagine situations for the characters. Some examples could be:

- We don't know much about Belize's life outside of the play. What is Belize's life with his boyfriend like? What would a meeting between Belize and his mother look like? What would he tell her about AIDS in New York seen from his position at the hospital? What would it be like if the Angel had, mistakenly perhaps, chosen Belize as a prophet?
- We are often treated to Harper's inner life. However, what would she say to Roy Cohn if she met him? What does her life in San Francisco look like? What would a scene between Harper and her mother, as described in the play, look like?
- After Hannah has her encounter with the Angel she clearly goes through a transformation into being the woman we meet in the epilogue. What situations between the end of the play and the epilogue changed her further?

• Roy Cohn visits Joe, who has moved to Washington, years later. What does he have to tell him? Giving the administration changed in 1992, how would Cohn describe this era?

Continuing these scenarios, create situations for each character and work on their reactions in situations outside of the text but within the universe of the play.

Writing/understanding the character
The longer speeches of the play present special challenges for actors. As a bridge between working on these speeches, characters and the themes, motives and politics of the play this writing exercise might be helpful.

• Considering that the scene between Louis and Belize in the coffee shop is central to both developing Louis's character and teasing out the different levels of politics engaged in the play, it might be a good place to intervene into other characters as well. Ask the actors to write the other characters' responses to Louis's political monologue.

  For example, in the scene we are represented with Belize's rebuttal in a round-about sort of way through his re-telling of the romance novel. However, what is Belize's political observation as we are introduced to it throughout the play – here you might want to read the coffee shop scene along with Louis/Belize at the Bethesda fountain scene?

  What would Joe say to Louis's theory of radical democracy?

  What would Prior say?

  What would the Angel as a symbol of the cosmology of stasis have to say?

  We are not told much about Harper's political point of view, indeed if she has one. What would she have to say to Louis's theory?

Repeat these questions of all characters. The actors should share these manifestos with each other and a group discussion should ensue about the characters. What are the different views of the different characters? What does that ultimately tell us about the play's visualization of a pluralistic and inclusive democracy in America?

- Following this, create improvised scenes between the characters using the same basic situation as Louis and Belize in the coffee shop.

The conflicts of the play

Many of the exercises above have also focused on exploring the themes and conflicts of the play by exploring the setting, language and characters. This exercise will be focused on working with the split scene technique.

Obviously the split scene technique is very important to the flow of the performance, but it also serves a thematic purpose by physically showing the audience how the lives of these characters become more and more intertwined. It also, of course, shows how the borders between usually separated worlds break down and chaos looms – the split scenes thus constitute a thematic comment. The split scenes allow the playwright to juxtapose elements that contrast or compliment each other. In *Millennium Approaches* act 3, scene 9, for example, is a scene in which the dialogue between the characters become completely intertwined as Louis is breaking up with Prior and Joe with Harper. Kushner says about the scene 'This should be fast and obviously furious; overlapping is fine; the proceedings may be a little confusing but not the final results' (82). In all acting being able to listen is essential, but in split scenes, such as this one, it is absolutely crucial as the actor is actually having a conversation not just with the immediate scene partner, but with the other two characters as well. However, before being able to listen it is necessary to be able to concentrate in a noisy or confusing situation. The following exercises can help doing that:

- Let two actors sit opposite each other and talk about separate topics that they choose. Each actor has to maintain their own argument and line of reason without being overtaken, engaged or drawn into the other person's line of reason. Slowly build up to having several couples talking around the stage (or room) simultaneously. Choose one person to lead the exercise. This person will clap and everybody will stop their argument. Then each time the leader points to a couple they'll start their argument again exactly where they left off, maintaining their energy. Several couples can be going at the same time, but must stop and start when the leader tells them to. As the actors get used to the exercise have them move around the stage/room as well adding a physical challenge to the concentration.

- Following this exercise; let pairs of actors improvise sets of split scenes with connection to the theme of the play. On one side of the stage a couple discuss, for example, affording health care while, on the other side, two politicians debate lowering taxes. On one side of the scene a man calls his mother to tell her he is gay, while, on the other side, a gay man tells his lover he has AIDS. On one side of the stage a woman is describing her longing for sex to a priest in her church while, on the other, a man discusses his erectile dysfunction with his doctor. The scenarios are endless.

- In a variation on this exercise the scenes can be developed individually before then being played out in split scene scenarios.

- Following the exercise go back to the actual split scene being worked on and use the same mechanisms to control the environment. While working on the scene you may want to go back to the 'reading exercises' and use these as well to play with the tone/rhythm/energy levels of the scene.

Winding down

Keeping in mind that *Angels in America* is written as a response, in a Brechtian fashion, to William Hoffman's *As Is*, it can be helpful for participants to write a response to the play or Kushner at the end of a workshop. In the quote at the beginning of this chapter Kushner talks about getting mad at a play. Ask yourself if there are elements of *Angels in America* that make you mad. If so, what are they? Why do they make you mad? Take these observations and create a piece of writing responding to that element of the play. This can take any form you would like; a short scene, a dialogue, a play, a monologue, a poem, a letter to Kushner, a letter to Harper, Prior, Louis, Joe, Hannah, Roy, Ethel, the Angel or any character.

If this last exercise is done at a workshop it can be a good idea to collect the pieces of writing and print them so the participants go home with a number of responses to the play.

Timeline 1945–1993

Politics

Culture

1945   House Un-American Committee becomes a standing committee in the United States Senate. In 1947 the Committee held hearings about alleged Communist infiltration of the Hollywood movie industry resulting in a black list of 'suspicious' artists; the USA detonates the world's first atomic bomb in New Mexico and later drops atomic bombs on Hiroshima and Nagasaki.

1947   Tennessee Williams's play *A Streetcar Named Desire* opens on Broadway; 10 October, Bertolt Brecht appears in front of the House Un-American Activities Committee claiming to never have been a member of the Communist Party. He leaves for East Germany the following day.

1949   The Soviet Union detonates its own atomic bomb.

Arthur Miller's *Death of a Salesman* opens on Broadway.

1950   Senator Joseph McCarthy of Wisconsin delivers a speech in which

Sunset Boulevard opens in movie theatres.

Politics

Culture

he claims to be in possession of a list
of Communists and spies within the
state department. McCarthy was to
become the face of the Communist
witch-hunt of the 1950s.

1951   The trial against Julius and
Ethel Rosenberg begins. The
Rosenbergs are tried for conspiracy
to deliver information regarding the
atomic bomb to the Soviet Union.

The film version of *A Streetcar
Named Desire* with Marlon Brando
and Vivien Leigh opens.

1953   Ethel and Julius Rosenberg
are executed in Sing Sing Prison in
upstate New York on 19 June.

1954   The first post-war production
of Brecht and Weill's *Threepenny
Opera* opens on Broadway.

1961   The Berlin Wall is
constructed.

1962   Edward Albee's *Who's Afraid
of Virginia Woolf* opens on Broadway;
a Cold War anti-Communist thriller,
The Manchurian Candidate, opens in
movie theatres.

1963   The March on Washington
for Jobs and Freedom takes place
organized by civil rights, labour and
religious movements. Dr Martin
Luther King delivers a speech in
which he utters the famous 'I have a
dream'; President John F. Kennedy is
assassinated.

Politics

Culture

1964   The Civil Rights Act, outlawing racial segregation in schools and public places, is passed in America.

1967   Charles Ludlam creates the Ridiculous Theatrical Company in New York City.

1968   Dr Martin Luther King, the American Civil Rights leader, is assassinated; Robert F. Kennedy (John F. Kennedy's brother) is assassinated campaigning to become the democratic nominee for president; Vietnam War protests are increasing; Riots break out outside the Democratic convention in Chicago, Illinois.

The Boys in the Band opens in New York as the first major commercially successful play about and with homosexual characters.

1969   The Stonewall Riots, June. When police tried to raid the Stonewall Inn, a gay bar, in the West Village in New York City, a group of drag queens and gay men actively resisted leading to a stand-off between the gay community and the authorities. This marks a turning point in the gay liberation struggle; escalation of Vietnam War Protests all over America and the world.

Judy Garland dies in June.

1970   Four students are shot dead at Kent State University by the Ohio National Guard during an anti-War protest highlighting the violent

Politics

Culture

division over the Vietnam War in
America; increasing civil unrest.

1975   Robert Altman's movie
Nashville opens in movie theatres:
Richard Schechner directs *Mother
Courage in* New York.

1976   Richard Foreman directs
Threepenny Opera in New York.

1980   Ronald Reagan is elected
president with George H. W. Bush as
vice-president. The two campaigned
on cutting taxes, a hard line policy
towards the Soviet Union, and re-
establishing so-called 'family values'.

1981 The first AIDS cases are
reported in the United States.

1982   The organization 'Gay Men's
Health Crisis' is established in New
York City to overcome the city's
inactivity towards people with AIDS;
AIDS is used for the first time.

Harvey Fierstein's play *Torch Song
Trilogy* opens on Broadway for a
3-year run, closing in 1985; *Cats*
opens on Broadway and runs for
8 years closing in 1990.

1983   Playwright Tennessee
Williams dies in New York; The
musical *La Cage Aux Folles*, with a
book by Harvey Fierstein, opens on
Broadway for a 4-year run. The
musical contains the song 'I am what
I am'.

1984   Ronald Reagan is re-elected
president of the USA.

Politics

Culture

1985 Reagan mentions AIDS
publicly for the first time in a
response to a reporter's question;
Mikhail Gorbachev becomes
General Secretary of the Communist
Party of the Soviet Union and begins
his policies of Glasnost and
Perestroika.

William Hoffman's *As Is* opens on
Broadway; Larry Kramer's *The
Normal Heart* opens at the Public
Theater in New York City; a made
for TV movie about AIDS, *An Early
Frost*, airs in America; Rock Hudson
dies of AIDS; Oskar Eustis directs
Kushner's *A Bright Room Called Day*.

1986 Roy Cohn dies of AIDS.

1987 President Reagan gives his
first major speech on AIDS.

1987 ACT UP, a gay protest
organization, is founded in New York
as a more radical protest movement
against the administration's
inactivity in AIDS policy; AZT is
approved by the FDA; USA blocks
immigrants and travellers with
AIDS from entering the country.

1988 George H. W. Bush is
elected president of the USA.

Tony Kushner starts working on
Angels in America.

1989 The Berlin Wall falls on
9 November. This is seen as a symbol
of the end of the Cold War.

1990 50,282 people are estimated
to have died of AIDS since the
beginning of the epidemic; Germany
is reunified; Ronald Reagan
apologizes for his neglect of the
epidemic while he was president;

First workshop production of
Angels in America at the Mark Taper
Forum in Los Angeles; the movie
Long Time Companion, with a
screen play by Craig Lucas, about
the impact of AIDS on a small

Politics

Culture

Queer Nation, a direct action organization, is founded in New York City to fight for GLBTQ visibility and politics.

group of friends opens in movie theatres.

1991   World premiere of *Millennium Approaches* at the Eureka Theatre in San Francisco.

1992   Bill Clinton is elected president campaigning among other things on allowing homosexuals to serve in the American military.

Millennium Approaches opens at the Royal National Theatre in London; *Millennium Approaches* and *Perestroika* performed as *Angels in America* at the Mark Taper Forum in Los Angeles.

1993   The 'Don't Ask, Don't Tell' policy is introduced as a compromise under which gay men and lesbians will be allowed to serve as long as they refrain from stating their sexuality publicly. The military then will refrain from asking. The bill is met with criticism from Gay and Lesbian organizations.

Angels in America is performed on Broadway; the movie *Philadelphia* opens in movie theatres.

References

All translations from the Danish and German are by me.

Abramovich, Alex (2003), 'Hurricane Kushner Hits the Heartland'. *New York Times*, 30 November.

Aronson, Arnold (1997), 'Design for *Angels in America*: Envisioning the Millennium', in Deborah R. Geis and Steven F. Kruger (eds), *Approaching the Millennium: Essays on Angels in America*. Ann Arbor: University of Michigan Press, pp. 213–226.

Benjamin, Walter (1968), *Illuminations: Essays and Reflections*, New York: Schocken Books.

Berman, Larry (1990), 'Looking Back on the Reagan Presidency', in Larry Berman (ed.), *Looking Back on the Reagan Presidency*. Baltimore: Johns Hopkins University Press, pp. 3–17.

Bigsby, Christopher (1999), *Contemporary American Playwrights*. New York: Cambridge University Press.

Borreca, Art (1997), 'Dramaturging the Dialectic: Brecht, Benjamin, and Declan Donnellan's Production of *Angels in America*', in Deborah R. Geis and Steven F. Kruger (eds), *Approaching the Millennium: Essays on Angels in America*. Ann Arbor: University of Michigan Press, pp. 245–260.

Brecht, Bertolt (1964), *Brecht on Theatre: The Development of an Aesthetic*. John Willett (ed.). New York: Hill and Wang.

Cadden, Michael (1997), 'Strange Angel: The Pinklisting of Roy Cohn', in Deborah R. Geis and Steven F. Kruger (eds), *Approaching the Millennium: Essays on Angels in America*. Ann Arbor: University of Michigan Press, pp.78–89.

Clum, John M. (2000), *Still Acting Gay: Male Homosexuality in Modern Drama*. First St Martin's Griffin Edition, New York: St Martin's Press.

Courdileone, K. A. (2000), '"Politics in an Age of Anxiety": Cold War Political Culture and the Crisis in American Masculinity, 1949–1960', in *The Journal of American History*. Vol. 87, No. 2 (September): 515–545.

Cunningham, Michael (1998), 'Thinking about Fabulousness', in Robert Vorlicky (ed.), *Tony Kushner in Conversation*. Ann Arbor: University of Michigan Press, pp. 62–76.

Davidson, Gordon (1998), 'A Conversation with Tony Kushner and Robert Altman', in Robert Vorlicky (ed.), *Tony Kushner in Conversation*. Ann Arbor: University of Michigan Press, pp. 128–147.

Epstein, Steven (1996), *Impure Science: AIDS, Activism, and the Politics of Knowledge*. Los Angeles: University of California Press.

Fisher, James (2002), *The Theater of Tony Kushner: Living Past Hope*, London: Routledge, 2002.

Frantzen, Allan J. (1997), 'Prior to the Normans: The Anglo-Saxons in *Angels in America*', in Deborah R. Geis and Steven F. Kruger (eds), *Approaching the Millennium: Essays on Angels in America*. Ann Arbor: University of Michigan Press, pp. 134–150.

Gorbachev, Mikhail (1987), *Perestroika: New Thinking for Our Country and the World*, New York: Harper and Row.

Gorchakov, N. M. (1954), *Stanislavsky Directs*. New York: Funk and Wagnalls Company.

Greenman, Ben (2003), 'Tony Kushner, Radical Pragmatist'. *Mother Jones*, November/December 2003.

Grenier, Cynthia (2003), 'Angels 2 still Rings Hollow but It Adds Powerful Scenes'. *Washington Times*, 12, December.

Holm, Bent (1995), 'Flying in Different Directions: American Angels in Denmark', in Per Brask (ed.), *Essays on Kushner's Angels*. Winnipeg: Blizzard Publishing, pp. 29–50.

Jones, Susan (1998), 'Tony Kushner's *Angels*', in Robert Vorlicky (ed.), *Tony Kushner in Conversation*. Ann Arbor: University of Michigan Press, pp. 157–169.

Krasner, David (2006), 'Stonewall, "Constant Historical Progress," and *Angels in America*: The Neo-Hegelian Positivist Sense', in James Fisher (ed.), *Tony Kushner: New Essays on the Art and Politics of the Plays*, Jefferson, NC: McFarland and Company.

Kushner, Tony (1995), *Thinking About the Longstanding Problems of Virtue and Happiness*. New York: Theatre Communications Group.

Kushner, Tony (1997), 'Notes about Political Theater', in *The Kenyon Review.* Vol. XIX, No. 3/4 (Summer/Fall): 19–34.

Lahr, John (1993), 'The Theatre: Earth Angels'. *New Yorker*, 1993.

Lund, Me (1995), 'Englenes Tilbagetog'. *Berlingske Tidende*, 12 February.

Mann, Thomas E. (1990), 'Thinking about the Reagan Years', in Larry Berman (ed.), *Looking Back on the Reagan Presidency*. Baltimore: Johns Hopkins University, pp. 18–29.

Mars-Jones, Adam (1998), 'Tony Kushner at the Royal National Theatre of Great Britain', in Robert Vorlicky (ed.), *Tony Kushner in Conversation*. Ann Arbor: University of Michigan Press, pp. 18–29.

Matsuoka, Amy Vaillancourt (2007), '"Angels" abide in director Ackerman's Japanese theatrical haven'. *The Daily Yomiuri*, 31 March.

Mauss, Armand L. (1994), 'Refuge and Retrenchment: The Mormon Quest for Identity', in Cornwall, Heaton and Young (eds.), *Contemporary Mormonism*, Urbana: University of Illinois Press.

McLeod, Bruce (1998), 'The Oddest Phenomena in Modern History', in Robert Vorlicky (ed.), *Tony Kushner in Conversation*. Ann Arbor: University of Michigan Press, pp. 77–84.

Meisner, Natalie (2003), 'Messing with the Idyllic: The Performance of Femininity in Kushner's *Angels in America*', in *The Yale Journal of Criticism*. Vol. 16, No.1: 177–189.

Minton, Gretchen E., and Schultz, Ray (2006), '*Angels in America*: Adapting to a New Medium in a New Millennium', in *American Drama* Vol. 15, No. 1 (Winter): 17–42.

Mizui, Yoko (1994), 'Kushner's "Angels" comes to Japan'. *The Daily Yomiuri*, 26 November.

Ogden, Daryl (2000), 'Cold War Science and the Body Politic: An Immuno/Virological Approach to *Angels in America*', in *Literature and Medicine* Vol. 19, No. 2 (Fall): 241–261.

Omer-Sherman, Ranen (2007), 'Jewish/Queer: Thresholds of Identity in Tony Kushner's *Angels in America*', in *Shofar: An Interdisciplinary Journal of Jewish Studies*. Vol. 25, No. 4: 78–98.

Pacheco, Patrick R. (1998), 'AIDS, Angels, Activism and Sex in the Nineties', in Robert Vorlicky (ed.), *Tony Kushner in Conversation*. Ann Arbor: University of Michigan Press, pp. 51–61.

Reinelt, Janelle (1997), 'Notes on Angels in America as American Epic Theater', in Deborah R. Geis and Steven F. Kruger (eds), *Approaching the Millennium: Essays on Angels in America*. Ann Arbor: University of Michigan Press, 234–244.

Rich, Frank (1992), 'Marching out of the Closet, into History'. *New York Times*, 10 November.

Rich, Frank (1993a), 'A New Generation on Old Broadway'. *New York Times*, 6 June.

Rich, Frank (1993b), 'A Play to Embrace all Possibilities in Art and Life'. *New York Times*, 5 May.

Richards, David (1993), '*Perestroika*, Part 2 of Tony Kushner's Huge Daring Drama Is Moving because It Is Humane'. *New York Times*, 28 November.

Rimmerman, Craig A. (1998), 'Presidency, U.S.', in Raymond A. Smith (ed.), *Encyclopedia of AIDS: A Social, Political, Cultural, and Scientific Record of the HIV Epidemic*. Chicago: Fitzroy Dearborn.

Román, David (1998), *Acts of Intervention: Performance, Gay Culture and AIDS*. Bloomington: Indiana University Press.

Savran, David (1996), 'Tony Kushner', interview with Tony Kushner in Phillip C. Kolin and Colby H. Kullman (eds), *Speaking on Stage: Interviews with Contemporary American Playwrights*. Tucaloosa: University of Alabama Press.

Savran, David (1997), 'Ambivalence, Utopia, and a Queer Sort of Materialism: How *Angels in America* Reconstructs the Nation', in Deborah R. Geis and Steven F. Kruger (eds), *Approaching the Millennium: Essays on Angels in America*. Ann Arbor: University of Michigan Press, pp.13–39.

Shilts, Randy (1987), *And the Band Played On: Politics, People, and the AIDS Epidemic*. New York: St Martin's Press.

Sinfield, Alan (1999), *Out on Stage: Lesbian and Gay Theatre in the Twentieth Century*. New Haven: Yale University Press.

Solomon, Alisa (1997), 'Wrestling with *Angels*': A Jewish Fantasia', in Deborah R. Geis and Steven F. Kruger (eds), *Approaching the Millennium: Essays on Angels in America*. Ann Arbor: University of Michigan Press, 118–133.

Spiegel, Hubert (1993), 'Engel ohne festen Wohnsit'. *Frankfurter Allgemeine Zeitung*, 30 September.

Stanislavski, Konstantin (1961), *Creating a Role*. New York: Theatre Arts Books, 1961.

Stevens, Andrea (1993), 'Finding a Devil within to Portray Roy Cohn'. *New York Times*, 18 April.

Sucher, C. Bernd (1992), 'Alles Unter Kondom? Tony Kushner's Angels in America Beim Europa-Theater-Festival in Dusseldorf'. *Sueddeutcsche Zeitung*, 21 November.

Sucher, C. Bernd (1993), 'Lederman trifft Fummeltrine'. *Sueddeutsche Zeitung*, 27 September.

Szentgyorgyi, Tom (1998), 'Look Back – and Forward – in Anger', in Robert Vorlicky (ed.), *Tony Kushner in Conversation*. Ann Arbor: University of Michigan Press, pp. 11–17.

Tanaka, Nobuko (2004a), 'Dreams with Wings'. *The Japan Times*, 11 February.

Tanaka, Nobuko (2004b), 'Timeless Message of Divine Angels Rings Loud and Clear'. *The Japan Times*, 11 February.

Uthmann, Joerg von (1993), 'Ein Engel kommt nach Sodom'. *Frankfurter Allgemeine Zeitung*, 13 May 1993.

Weber, Bruce (1993), '*Angels'* Angels'. *New York Times Magazine*, 25 April.

Weber, Bruce (1994a), 'On Stage, and Off'. *New York Times*, 7 January.

Weber, Bruce (1994b), 'Two Wings, a Prayer, and Backstage Help'. *New York Times*, 5 January.

Wille, Franz (1995), 'Historical Revue and Dance of Death', in Per Brask, *Essays on Kushner's Angels*. Winnipeg: Blizzard Publishing, pp. 52–61.

Further Reading

The play

Kushner, Tony, *Angels in America: A Gay Fantasia on National Themes*, New York: Theatre Communications Group 1995. The plays were published individually in 1992 and 1993. This book quotes from the first combined paperback edition from 2003. No significant changes have been made to the original text.

The 2003 HBO TV production of the play is available on DVD. It has a screenplay by Tony Kushner, is directed by Mike Nichols and stars among others Meryl Streep, Emma Thompson and Al Pacino.

The playwright and the play

Bigsby, Christopher, *Contemporary American Playwrights*, New York: Cambridge University Press, 1999. Provides an analysis of significant contemporary American playwrights, among them Tony Kushner. Serves as an excellent introduction to Kushner's work and enables the reader view Kushner in relation to his contemporaries.

Brask, Per (ed.), *Essays on Tony Kushner's Angels*, Winnipeg: Blizzard Publishing, 1995. An early collection of essays on *Angels in America*. Particularly useful for its essays on the Danish, German and Australian productions of the play. It also offers an interview with Tony Kushner by David Savran which is a good introduction to Kushner's theory of the fabulous.

Fisher, James, *The Theater of Tony Kushner: Living Past Hope*, London: Routledge, 2002. The only study of Kushner's general production. Fisher offers an excellent analysis of Kushner's theatre and the book allows the reader to see *Angels in America* in relation to Kushner's work as such. The chapter on *Angels in America* will be helpful for any student working with the play.

Fisher, James (ed.), *Tony Kushner: New Essays on the Art and Politics of the Plays*, Jefferson, NC: McFarland & Company Inc. Publishers, 2006. The most recent collection of essays analysing and assessing Kushner's work. The variety of essays offers readings of Kushner's plays and the multitude of sources influencing them.

Geis, Deborah R., and Kruger, Steven F. (eds), *Approaching the Millennium: Essays on Angels in America*, Ann Arbor: University of Michigan Press, 1997. The canonical collection of essays on *Angels in America*. It contains essays by leading theatre scholars and highlights social, religious, racial, political and textual theories and their working within the play. Any serious study of the play must consider the ideas raised in these essays.

Kushner, Tony, *Thinking about the Longstanding Problems of Virtue and Happiness: Essays, a Play, Two Poems, and a Prayer*, New York: Theatre Communications Group, 1995. This highly readable collection of essays will allow the student of *Angels in America* to become familiar with Kushner's thoughts on sex, America and politics – all topics addressed in *Angels in America*. It also contains the play *Slavs*.

Kushner, Tony, 'Notes about Political Theater', in the *Kenyon Review*. Volume XIX, No. 3/4, (Summer/Fall 1997). This short article constitutes Kushner's successful attempt at defining his own political theatre practice. For the reader interested in the political aspects of *Angels in America* or political theatre in general the article is essential.

Mendelsohn, Daniel, 'Winged Messages', in *The New York Review of Books*, Volume 51, No. 2 (12 February 2004). This short article reads the HBO production of *Angels in America* into a larger American and contemporary context. It will be helpful in a study attempting to compare the stage play with the TV version.

Minton, Gretchen E., and Schultz, Ray, '*Angels in America*: Adapting to a New Medium in a New Millennium', in *American Drama*. Volume 15, No. 1 (Winter 2006). Like Daniel Mendelsohn's article this article compares the stage and TV versions of the play. It conducts a thorough textual analysis of the changes made to the script and reads these absences as political.

Cultural context

Berman, Larry (ed.), *Looking Back on the Reagan Presidency*, Baltimore: Johns Hopkins University Press, 1990. A collection of essays by political scientists and historians evaluating the Reagan presidency and its consequences. For the most part fairly balanced, the articles highlight different aspects of the presidency and its politics.

Bigsby, Christopher, *A Critical Introduction to Twentieth Century American Drama: Volume Three, beyond Broadway*, New York: Cambridge University Press, 1985. Where Bigsby's other work on the modern American drama focuses on the established theatre, primarily Broadway and established Off Broadway writers, this volume focuses on the avant-garde or alternative theatre. It offers a very readable introduction to most of the experimental artists that Kushner is inspired by.

Bigsby, Christopher, *Modern American Drama 1945–1990*, New York: Cambridge University Press, 1992. As a very readable study of the dramatic works of American canonical writers such as O'Neill, Williams and Albee this volume easily serves as an introduction to the American playwriting tradition that Kushner is both part and re-newer of.

Brecht, Bertolt, *Brecht on Theatre: The Development of an Aesthetic*, John Willett (ed.), New York: Hill and Wang, 1964. This collection of writings on the theatre by Brecht contains important pieces such as, *A Short Organum for the Theatre*, *The Modern Theatre Is the Epic Theatre*, *The Street Scene*, *New Technique of Acting* and *Stage Design of the Epic Theatre*. Most of these pieces are short and fairly easy to read for the student interested in how Kushner is inspired by Brecht's theories of the epic theatre.

John M. Clum, *Still Acting Gay: Male Homosexuality in Modern Drama*, first St Martin's Griffin edition, New York: St Martin's Griffin, 2000. Like Alan Sinfield, Clum offers an overview of particularly American gay theatre history with a focus on the mainstream theatre.

Román, David, *Acts of Intervention: Performance, Gay Culture and AIDS*, Bloomington: Indiana University Press, 1998. Where most other gay theatre histories focus on the more established theatre's reaction to the AIDS crisis Román's work analyses the gay community's use of the theatre as strategy and art in the face of AIDS. Very readable it allows the reader to contextualize *Angels in America* and analyse its differences and similarities with other gay theatre. It also has a study of the Los Angeles performance of the play in relation to the change of American politics around the time of the opening.

Savran, David, *A Queer Sort of Materialism: Recontextualizing American Theater*, Ann Arbor: University of Michigan Press, 2003. A collection of essays that will help the more advanced student contextualize *Angels in America*. Besides containing Savran's seminal study of the play the book contains an excellent article on theatre as 'the Queerest art' also drawing on *Angels in America*.

Shilts, Randy, *And the Band Played On: Politics, People, and the AIDS epidemic*, New York: St Martin's Press, 1987. This journalistic account of the early AIDS crisis in America is a thorough and troubling study of the events. It allows the reader to follow the development month by month and constructs a thorough, if partisan, look at the events unfolding at the time of *Angels in America*.

Sinfield, Alan, *Out on Stage: Lesbian and Gay Theatre in the Twentieth Century*, New Haven: Yale University Press, 1999. A thorough study of the theatrical representation of lesbians and gay men in England and America, it offers the reader a very readable and socially critical account of gay theatre history.

Smith, Raymond A. (ed.), *Encyclopedia of AIDS: A Social, Political, Cultural, and Scientific Record of the HIV Epidemic*, Chicago: Fitzroy Dearborn, 1998. An excellent resource on all questions related to AIDS both in terms of the disease itself and its cultural and political context.

Interviews with Tony Kushner

Savran, David, 'Tony Kushner', in Phillip C. Kolin and Colby H. Kullman (eds), *Speaking on Stage: Interviews with Contemporary American Playwrights*, Tuscaloosa: University of Alabama Press, 1996. A very informative and insightful interview with Tony Kushner addressing his background, theories of the theatre, *Angels in America* and politics.

Vorlicky, Robert (ed.), *Tony Kushner in Conversation*, Ann Arbor: University of Michigan Press, 1998. This collection of 21 interviews with Kushner is an indispensable resource when studying his work and particularly *Angels in America*. Kushner has been interviewed on multiple issues and all are addressed in this collection giving the reader insight into his theories, background, work process and relation to history (American and gay).

Documentary

Wrestling with Angels by filmmaker Freida Lee Mock is an excellent and prize winning documentary about Tony Kushner's life and work centring around his political stances, his homosexuality and Jewish heritage. It is a great introduction – partly through some of the many artists who have worked with him – to the larger oeuvre of Kushner and allows the viewer to see *Angels in America* in a larger both political and theatrical context. See: www.wrestlingwithangelsthemovie.com

Index